Soup
Favourites

Paré • Pirk • Billey • Darcy

Distributed by
Canada Book Distributors
www.canadabookdistributors.com
www.companyscoming.com
Tel: 1-800-661-9017

Library and Archives Canada Cataloguing in Publication

Title: Soup favourites / Paré, Pirk, Billey, Darcy.
Other titles: Company's Coming
Names: Paré, Jean, author. | Pirk, Wendy, 1973- author. | Billey, Ashley, author. | Darcy, James, 1956- author.
Description: Includes index.
Identifiers: Canadiana 20190186453 | ISBN 9781772070453 (softcover)
Subjects: LCSH: Soups. | LCGFT: Cookbooks.
Classification: LCC TX757 .P37 2020 | DDC 641.81/3—dc23

Cover: ALLEKO/GettyImages; Company's Coming

All inside photos by Company's Coming except: from Gettyimages: AlexPro9500, 125; ALLEKO, 51, 79; bhofack2, 87; bonchan, 103, 105, 151; cobraphoto, 47, 97; czarny_bez, 19; Dzonsli, 81; Ezumelmages, 37; ginauf, 53; jreika, 75; Juefraphoto, 139; JuliScalzi, 157; kabVisio, 55; LynneMitchell, 29; margouillatphotos, 153; Mariha-kitchen, 59; martinturzak, 45, 49, 109; Mizina, 1, 85; nebari, 23; PingPongCat, 69; RafotografZ, 83; Rebekah Flory, 43; Rimma_Bondarenko, 145; sgame, 155; Szakaly, 77; Ulyashka, 95; Vanillaechoes, 137; VezzaniPhotography, 27; Zoonar/D.Dzinnik, 119.

We acknowledge the financial support of the Government of Canada.
Nous reconnaissons l'appui financier du gouvernement du Canada.

Funded by the Government of Canada
Financé par le gouvernement du Canada | Canadä

PC: 38-1

Table of Contents

The Jean Paré Story

Jean Paré (pronounced "jeen PAIR-ee") grew up understanding that the combination of family, friends and home cooking is the best recipe for a good life. When Jean left home, she took with her a love of cooking, many family recipes and an intriguing desire to read cookbooks as if they were novels!

"Never share a recipe you wouldn't use yourself."

When her four children had all reached school age, Jean volunteered to cater the 50th anniversary celebration of the Vermilion School of Agriculture, now Lakeland College, in Alberta, Canada. Working from her home, Jean prepared a dinner for more than 1,000 people and from there launched a flourishing catering operation that continued for more than 18 years.

As requests for her recipes increased, Jean was often asked, "Why don't you write a cookbook?" The release of *150 Delicious Squares* on April 14, 1981, marked the debut of what would soon turn into one of the world's most popular cookbook series.

Company's Coming cookbooks are distributed in Canada, the United States, Australia and other world markets. Bestsellers many times over in English, Company's Coming cookbooks have also been published in French and Spanish.

Familiar and trusted in home kitchens around the world, Company's Coming cookbooks are offered in a variety of formats. Highly regarded as kitchen workbooks, the softcover Original Series, with its lay-flat plastic comb binding, is still a favourite among home cooks.

Jean Paré's approach to cooking has always called for quick and easy recipes using everyday ingredients. That view served her well, and the tradition continues in the Practical Gourmet series.

Jean's Golden Rule of Cooking is: Never share a recipe you wouldn't use yourself. It's an approach that has worked—millions of times over!

Introduction

A homemade bowl of soup goes a long way to curing what ails you. Remember the magical healing powers of Mom's chicken soup, lovingly administered, when you were in bed with a cold? It wasn't long after that you started feeling better and were back on your feet. And whether it's a hearty chowder or a delicate brothy dish, all soups contain a little of that same comforting goodness.

Comforting qualities aside, one of the best things about homemade soups is their versatility. As long as you have a well-stocked spice rack, fresh or frozen veggies on hand, meat in the freezer or legumes, rice or pasta in the pantry, you can whip up a steaming pot of goodness. It needn't be difficult or complicated.

The secret to a truly excellent soup is in the broth. You can use the freshest, best-tasting ingredients in your soup and still be disappointed in the end result if you've added them to a tasteless broth. A good broth gives your soup a complexity and depth of flavour that will have diners reaching for the ladle to serve themselves a second bowl.

Stock vs. Broth

Although many people use these two terms interchangeably, there is a difference between stock and broth.

Stock is made by boiling bones, with or without meat, for many hours (think 5 to 8) until the collagen in the bones is released. The flavour comes from the bones, and the end result is thicker than broth and slightly gelatinous. Stock is used as a base to build flavour in gravies and sauces as well as in soups and stews; it is generally not consumed on its own.

Broth is made by boiling meat and bones with aromatic vegetables such as garlic, onion and carrots (or only vegetables for a vegetarian broth). It has a shorter cooking time and more seasonings. Because it is so well seasoned and flavourful, broth can be consumed on its own, although it can also build flavour in soups, stews and many side dishes.

Broth Basics

To build flavour in your broth, sauté your onions and other aromatic vegetables together until they begin to release their moisture before adding liquid. Cooking the veggies first allows their flavours to really develop.

If you find your broth to be a bit lackluster, there are a number of things you can add to give it a flavour boost. A few dashes of soy sauce or hoisin might help give the broth some depth; the soaking liquid of dried shitake mushrooms or a cheese rind will add a touch of umami that could be just what your broth needs; even a dollop of pesto or tomato paste can go a long way to transforming the flavour profile of your broth.

Tips for Superb Soups

A pot of soup is a great way to use up leftovers, but it's not an opportunity to resurrect suspicious-looking items in the refrigerator. Remember that excellent ingredients make excellent soup, in terms of both flavour and nutrition.

A fatty soup is not a yummy soup. Trim the fat off any meat you use or drain the fat if you are searing the meat before adding it to the soup. You can further reduce fat by placing a coffee filter on the soup's surface and blotting it up. Or if you don't need it right away, allow the soup to chill in the refrigerator. The fat will harden on the surface, making it easy to lift out.

When adding ingredients to your soup, consider their cooking times before tossing everything into the pot. Carrots take much longer to cook than zucchini, so do not add them at the same time unless you like your zucchini to be a mushy mess. Stagger ingredients according to how long they take to cook and be careful not to overcook or undercook them. Hard chunks of raw potato in a soup can be just as off-putting as mushy zucchini.

Most soup recipes can be doubled with no trouble, so you can make extra soup to freeze for later. Just make sure you use a pot large enough to accommodate the extra ingredients.

Thickening Tricks

Creamy, rich soups are a feast for the eyes as well as the taste buds. But not all soups are thickened with cream. There are several ways of thickening your soup:

• To make a roux, heat butter or other fat then sprinkle an equal amount of flour over it. Cook the flour in the fat and slowly stir in the liquid. Continual stirring or whisking eliminates any lumps. Once the mixture comes to a boil, reduce the heat to a simmer to allow the soup to thicken. Sauté mushrooms, onions or other vegetables in the butter before adding the flour.

• A slurry, a mixture of cold liquid with flour or cornstarch, can also be used to thicken a soup. Slowly add the slurry to the soup, stirring constantly while bringing it to a boil, and then reduce the heat. Over-boiling cornstarch will cause it to separate again.

- Make a purée with a portion of the soup and stir it back into the pot for a low-fat creamy texture.

- Add mashed potatoes or pureed beans to a soup to thicken it. This works especially well with chowders.

Note: Make sure to gently cook roux and slurries several minutes to eliminate the taste of raw flour.

Equipment

The scoop on soup is that you don't need a lot of fancy tools to simmer up some savoury fare. Usually, a large cooking pot is all that's required. We used a 4 1/2 quart (4.5 L) Dutch oven for most of our recipes.

Stock pot—Making stock from scratch, however, calls for a larger vessel to hold the bones, vegetables and liquid. An 8 quart (8 L) stockpot is ideal. Not only is it perfect for making delicious stocks, but it can also handle stews, sauces, blanching, boiling and steaming, especially if you're doubling recipes.

Hand blender—Useful for puréeing soups without having to remove hot liquids in batches to an upright blender.

Soup skimmer—This looks like a large, flat, perforated spoon. It's handy for skimming off foam when you're making the stock. Skimming off the foam will prevent your soup from becoming cloudy.

Small squares of cheesecloth and pieces of string—These allow you to wrap and tie specific herbs and spices into a bundle called a bouquet garni. By tying the other end of your string to your pot handle, you can easily pull out the herb package after cooking. For a reusable bouquet garni option, use a tea infuser or tea ball instead of cheesecloth to hold your herbs and spices.

Freezer Tips

Freeze homemade stock and broth in different sized containers to flavour not just soups but gravies, sauces, polenta, rice and other dishes. For tiny amounts, freeze in ice cube trays then transfer the cubes to a plastic freezer bag.

Use airtight containers to reduce freezer burn.

Freeze individual serving–sized portions of soup for an easy lunch option or for those nights when you want a comforting meal but just don't have the time to cook.

Certain ingredients, specifically potatoes and pasta, do not freeze well. Consider adding these ingredients after thawing. Undercook rice before freezing, as it will soften.

Soups thickened with dairy products, flour or cornstarch may separate when frozen. Whisk the soup while heating it to allow it to blend together again.

Garnishes of yogurt, sour cream and mayonnaise do not freeze well. Add these just before serving.

Classic Beef Barley Soup

Boiling the bones along with the meat gives stock a real richness and depth of flavour. This stock needs a long simmering time to really develop its flavours, though, so plan accordingly. If you need your soup on the table quickly, this isn't the dish for you. But if you have the time, this soup is definitely worth the wait.

Beef neck bones	3 lbs.	1.4 kg
Bone-in beef shanks	1 lb.	454 g
Cold water	16 cups	4 L
Celery ribs, with leaves, halved	6	6
Medium onions, halved	2	2
Medium carrot, halved	1	1
Bay leaves	2	2
Whole black peppercorns	10	10
Diced peeled potato	2 cups	500 mL
Garlic cloves	2	2
Can of crushed tomatoes (28 oz., 796 mL)	1	1
Chopped onion	1 cup	250 mL
Chopped celery	1 cup	250 mL
Diced carrot	1 cup	250 mL
Diced parsnip (optional)	1 cup	250 mL
Pearl barley	2/3 cup	150 mL
Brown sugar	1 tbsp.	15 mL
Cider vinegar	2 tsp.	10 mL
Salt	1 tsp.	5 mL
Pepper	3/4 tsp.	4 mL

For the stock, bring first 3 ingredients to a boil in a large pot. Boil, uncovered, for 5 minutes without stirring. Skim and discard foam from side of pot.

Stir in next 5 ingredients. Reduce heat to medium-low. Simmer, partially covered, for about 4 hours, stirring occasionally, until beef starts to fall off bones. Remove from heat. Transfer bones and shanks to a cutting board using a slotted spoon. Remove beef from bones. Discard bones. Chop beef coarsely and set aside. Strain stock through a sieve into a separate large pot. Discard solids.

For the soup, add remaining 12 ingredients to stock in pot. Bring to a boil. Add beef and reduce heat to medium-low. Simmer, partially covered, for about 45 minutes, stirring occasionally, until barley and vegetables are tender. Makes about 14 cups (3.5 L).

1 cup (250 mL): 220 Calories; 6 g Total Fat (2.5 g Mono, 0 g Poly, 2 g Sat); 55 mg Cholesterol; 18 g Carbohydrate (4 g Fibre, 3 g Sugar); 22 g Protein; 270 mg Sodium

Pot Roast Soup

All the flavours of a traditional pot roast dinner in a rich, stew-like soup loaded with tender meat and vegetables. Serve with fresh crusty bread or buns on the side to sop up the thick broth.

Cooking oil	2 tsp.	10 mL
Stewing beef	1 lb.	454 g
Chopped onion	1 cup	250 mL
Garlic cloves, minced (or 1/2 tsp., 2 mL, powder)	2	2
Prepared beef broth	5 cups	1.25 L
Cubed peeled potato	2 cups	500 mL
Baby carrots, halved	1 cup	250 mL
Tomato paste (see Tip, page 18)	1 tbsp.	15 mL
Worcestershire sauce	1 tbsp.	15 mL
Dried thyme	1/4 tsp.	1 mL
Salt	1/4 tsp.	1 mL
Water	1/4 cup	60 mL
All-purpose flour	1/4 cup	60 mL
Frozen peas	1 cup	250 mL

Heat cooking oil in a large saucepan on medium-high. Add beef and cook for about 10 minutes, stirring often, until browned. Reduce heat to medium. Add onion and garlic. Cook for 3 to 5 minutes, stirring occasionally, until onion is softened.

Stir in broth and bring to a boil. Reduce heat to medium-low. Simmer, partially covered, for about 40 minutes until beef is tender.

Stir in next 6 ingredients and bring to a boil.

Stir water into flour in a small bowl until smooth. Slowly add to soup, stirring constantly, until boiling and thickened. Reduce heat to medium. Boil gently, covered, for 15 to 20 minutes, stirring occasionally, until vegetables are tender.

Add peas. Heat, stirring, for 3 to 5 minutes until peas are tender. Makes 6 servings.

1 serving: 260 Calories; 8 g Total Fat (3.5 g Mono, 1 g Poly, 2.5 g Sat); 40 mg Cholesterol; 25 g Carbohydrate (3 g Fibre, 7 g Sugar); 21 g Protein; 820 mg Sodium

Burger Bean Soup

This hearty soup can be made ahead and is a perfect choice for busy weekday nights. Make it the evening before and pull it from the fridge to gently reheat. This soup also freezes beautifully.

Cooking oil	1 tbsp.	15 mL
Lean ground beef	1 1/2 lbs.	680 g
Chopped onion	2 cups	500 mL
Bacon slices, diced	6	6
Can of crushed tomatoes (28 oz., 796 mL, each)	1	1
Cans of kidney beans (14 oz., 398 mL, each), rinsed and drained	2	2
Medium carrots, thinly sliced	5	5
Medium peeled potatoes, cubed	5	5
Garlic cloves, minced	2	2
Brown sugar	1 tbsp.	15 mL
Cider vinegar	2 tsp.	10 mL
Celery salt	1 tsp.	5 mL
Pepper	1/2 tsp.	2 mL

Heat cooking oil in a large frying pan on medium-high. Add next 3 ingredients and scramble-fry for about 10 minutes until beef is no longer pink. Drain.

Combine remaining 9 ingredients in a large saucepan. Stir in beef mixture and bring to a boil. Reduce heat to medium-low and simmer, covered, for about 1 1/4 hours until vegetables are tender. Makes about 12 cups (3 L).

1 cup (250 mL): 340 Calories; 18 g Total Fat (8 g Mono, 2 g Poly, 6 g Sat); 45 mg Cholesterol; 25 g Carbohydrate (6 g Fibre, 4 g Sugar); 18 g Protein; 360 mg Sodium

Beef Pho

One of the great things about pho is that once you've perfected the broth, you can garnish it with your favourite ingredients to customize your bowl to your liking. Bean sprouts, fresh herbs such as mint, cilantro and Thai basil, fresh sliced chilies and lime wedges are all excellent garnish choices.

Medium rice stick noodles	1/2 lb.	225 g
Cooking oil	2 tsp.	10 mL
Thinly sliced onion	1 1/4 cups	300 mL
Water	4 cups	1 L
Prepared beef broth	4 cups	1 L
Cinnamon stick (4 inches, 10 cm)	1	1
Piece of ginger root (3 inch, 7.5 cm, length), halved	1	1
Star anise	1	1
Beef sirloin steak, thinly sliced (see Tip, page 32)	1 lb.	454 g
Fish sauce	2 tbsp.	30 mL
Granulated sugar	2 tbsp.	30 mL
Bean sprouts, trimmed	2 cups	500 mL
Thinly sliced red onion	1/2 cup	125 mL
Thinly sliced green onion	1/3 cup	75 mL

Cover noodles with hot water and let stand, covered, for 25 minutes until softened. Drain noodles and transfer to 6 serving bowls.

Heat cooking oil in a Dutch oven on medium-high. Add onion and cook for 5 minutes until browned.

Add water, stirring constantly and scraping any brown bits from bottom of pan for 1 minute. Add next 4 ingredients, reduce heat to medium-low and simmer for 15 minutes. Discard solids.

Stir in next 3 ingredients. Cooking, stirring, until beef has reached desired doneness.

Scatter remaining 3 ingredients over noodles, cover with beef and pour broth over top. Makes 6 servings.

1 serving: 360 Calories; 9 g Total Fat (3.5 g Mono, 1 g Poly, 3 g Sat); 35 mg Cholesterol; 35 g Carbohydrate (2 g Fibre, 7 g Sugar); 19 g Protein; 920 mg Sodium

Hearty Wild Rice Soup

Earthy mushrooms and a pleasant hint of tarragon complement the nutty flavour of wild rice. The grated carrot adds a little splash of colour.

Cooking oil	2 tsp.	10 mL
Chopped fresh white mushrooms	2 cups	500 mL
Lean ground beef	1 lb.	454 g
Chopped onion	1 cup	250 mL
Dried tarragon	1 tsp.	5 mL
All-purpose flour	3 tbsp.	45 mL
Prepared beef broth	6 cups	1.5 L
Wild rice	2/3 cup	150 mL
Grated carrot	1/2 cup	125 mL

Heat cooking oil in a large saucepan on medium. Add next 4 ingredients and scramble-fry for about 10 minutes until beef is no longer pink. Drain.

Sprinkle with flour. Heat, stirring, for 1 minute.

Stir in broth and rice and bring to a boil. Reduce heat to medium-low. Simmer, covered, for about 50 minutes, stirring occasionally, until rice is tender.

Stir in carrot. Cook, uncovered, for about 2 minutes, stirring often, until carrot is tender-crisp. Skim any fat from surface of soup (see Tip, below). Makes about 8 cups (2 L).

1 cup (250 mL): 170 Calories; 4.5 g Total Fat (1.5 g Mono, 1 g Poly, 1.5 g Sat); 35 mg Cholesterol; 17 g Carbohydrate (2 g Fibre, 3 g Sugar); 17 g Protein; 560 mg Sodium

Tip: To reduce the amount of fat in your soup, place a coffee filter on the soup's surface and blot the fat up. Or place the soup in the refrigerator to chill. The fat will harden on the surface, making it easy to scoop out.

Easy Beef Vegetable Soup

In this dish, we keep things simple by using prepared broth in place of a homemade stock. Loaded with ground beef, mushrooms, potato and barley, this filling soup is the perfect remedy to a cold winter's day.

Cooking oil	2 tsp.	10 mL
Extra-lean ground beef	1/2 lb.	225 g
Sliced fresh white mushrooms	1/2 cup	125 mL
Chopped onion	1/2 cup	125 mL
Chopped celery	1/2 cup	125 mL
All-purpose flour	2 tsp.	10 mL
Prepared beef broth	6 cups	1.5 L
Sliced carrot	1 cup	250 mL
Chopped peeled potato	1 cup	250 mL
Pearl barley	1/3 cup	75 mL
Tomato paste, optional (see Tip, below)	2 tbsp.	30 mL
Pepper	1/4 tsp.	1 mL
Half-and-half cream	2/3 cup	150 mL

Heat cooking oil in a large saucepan on medium. Add next 4 ingredients and scramble-fry for about 10 minutes until beef is no longer pink.

Sprinkle with flour. Heat, stirring, for 1 minute.

Add next 6 ingredients and bring to a boil. Reduce heat to medium-low. Simmer, partially covered, for about 1 hour, stirring occasionally, until barley and vegetables are tender and soup is thickened.

Add cream. Heat, stirring, for 1 to 2 minutes until heated through. Makes about 7 cups (1.75 L).

1 cup (250 mL): 170 Calories; 6 g Total Fat (2 g Mono, 1 g Poly, 2.5 g Sat); 30 mg Cholesterol; 19 g Carbohydrate (3 g Fibre, 1 g Sugar); 11 g Protein; 660 mg Sodium

Tip: If a recipe calls for less than an entire can of tomato paste, freeze the unopened can for 30 minutes. Open both ends and push the contents through one end. Slice off only what you need. Freeze the remaining paste in a resealable freezer bag or plastic wrap for future use.

Spiced Beef Soup

This rich soup, seasoned with cumin, coriander and ginger, pairs perfectly with fresh naan or crisp pappadums.

Cooking oil	1 tbsp.	15 mL
Beef stew meat, cut into 1/2 inch (12 mm) pieces	3/4 lb.	340 g
Cooking oil	2 tsp.	10 mL
Chopped onion	1 1/2 cups	375 mL
Ground cumin	2 tsp.	10 mL
Ground coriander	2 tsp.	10 mL
Ground ginger	1 tsp.	5 mL
Dried crushed chilies	1 tsp.	5 mL
Can of diced tomatoes (with juice) (28 oz., 796 mL)	1	1
Low-sodium prepared beef broth	4 cups	1 L
Can of chickpeas (19 oz., 540 mL), rinsed and drained	1	1
Medium zucchini (with peel), chopped	1	1
Chopped fresh mint leaves (or 1 1/2 tsp., 7 mL, dried)	2 tbsp.	30 mL
Liquid honey	2 tsp.	10 mL
Grated lemon zest	1 tsp.	5 mL

Heat first amount of cooking oil in a large pot or Dutch oven on medium-high. Add beef and cook for 5 to 10 minutes, stirring occasionally, until browned. Transfer to a large bowl and cover to keep warm.

Heat second amount of cooking oil in same large pot on medium. Add onion and cook for 5 to 10 minutes, stirring often, until softened.

Add next 4 ingredients and cook, stirring, for about 1 minute until fragrant.

Stir in beef, tomatoes and broth and bring to a boil on medium-high. Reduce heat to medium-low. Simmer, covered, for 20 minutes, stirring occasionally.

Stir in chickpeas. Simmer, covered, for about 20 minutes until beef is very tender.

Stir in remaining 4 ingredients. Cook, uncovered, on medium for about 5 minutes until zucchini is tender. Makes 8 servings.

1 serving: 200 Calories; 7 g Total Fat (2 g Mono, 2 g Poly, 1 g Sat); 19 mg Cholesterol; 4 g Carbohydrate (7 g Fibre, 15 g Sugar); 15 g Protein; 640 mg Sodium

French Onion Soup

*This soup has delicious caramelized onions and a definite herb undertone.
Remind everyone—the bowls are hot!*

Butter (or hard margarine)	2 tbsp.	30 mL
Medium onions, thinly sliced	8	8
Salt	1 tsp.	5 mL
Garlic cloves, minced (or 1 tsp., 5 mL, powder)	4	4
Coarsely ground pepper (or 1/4 tsp., 1 mL, pepper)	1/2 tsp.	2 mL
Dry sherry	1/2 cup	125 mL
Prepared beef broth	4 cups	1 L
Bay leaves	3	3
Sprigs of fresh thyme	3	3
Baguette slices, about 1/3 inch (1 cm) thick, lightly toasted or air-dried	4	4
Grated Gruyère cheese	1 1/3 cups	325 mL

Melt butter in a large saucepan on medium-low. Stir in onion and salt.
Cook, covered, for about 45 minutes, stirring occasionally, until onion is
softened but still white.

Stir in garlic and pepper. Cook, uncovered, on medium-high, for 5 to
10 minutes, stirring often, until onion is caramelized.

Add sherry and cook, scraping any brown bits from bottom of pan, until
combined.

Stir in next 3 ingredients and bring to a boil. Reduce heat to medium-low.
Simmer, covered, for 30 minutes, without stirring. Remove and discard bay
leaves and thyme sprigs.

Arrange 4 ovenproof bowls on a baking sheet with sides. Ladle into soup
bowls and place 1 slice of bread in each bowl. Sprinkle with cheese. Broil
on centre rack in oven for 3 to 5 minutes until cheese is melted and golden.
Let stand for 5 minutes. Carefully transfer hot soup bowls to plates. Makes
4 servings.

*1 serving: 370 Calories; 18 g Total Fat (6 g Mono, 2.5 g Poly, 8 g Sat); 40 mg Cholesterol;
32 g Carbohydrate (4 g Fibre, 11 g Sugar); 16 g Protein; 1480 mg Sodium*

Hearty Goulash Soup

Traditional goulash is enhanced with smoky bacon and harvest vegetables.
Served with fresh bread and red wine, it makes a satisfying fall dinner.

Bacon slices, diced	8	8
All-purpose flour	3 tbsp.	45 mL
Boneless beef cross rib (or blade) steak, trimmed of fat, cut into 3/4 inch (2 cm) cubes	1 lb.	454 g
Chopped onion	2 cups	500 mL
Garlic cloves, minced (or 3/4 tsp., 4 mL, powder)	3	3
Dry (or alcohol-free) red wine	1 cup	250 mL
Can of diced tomatoes (28 oz., 796 mL), with juice	1	1
Prepared beef broth	2 cups	500 mL
Diced peeled potato	1 1/2 cups	375 mL
Diced carrot	1 cup	250 mL
Diced parsnip	1 cup	250 mL
Can of tomato paste (5 1/2 oz., 156 mL)	1	1
Smoked (sweet) paprika	1 tsp.	5 mL
Salt	1/2 tsp.	2 mL
Pepper	1/4 tsp.	1 mL

Cook bacon in a large frying pan on medium until crisp. Transfer with a slotted spoon to a 3 1/2 to 4 quart (3.5 to 4 L) slow cooker. Drain and discard all but 1 tbsp. (15 mL) drippings.

Put flour into a large resealable freezer bag. Add beef. Seal bag and toss until beef is coated. Add beef to frying pan on medium. Discard any remaining flour. Cook for about 5 minutes, stirring occasionally, until browned. Transfer to slow cooker.

Add onion and garlic to frying pan. Cook for about 10 minutes, stirring often, until onion starts to soften and brown.

Add wine. Cook, stirring and scraping any brown bits from bottom of pan, until boiling. Pour over beef.

Stir in remaining 9 ingredients. Cook, covered, on Low for 9 to 10 hours or on High for 4 1/2 to 5 hours. Makes about 10 cups (2.5 L).

1 cup (250 mL): 390 Calories; 22 g Total Fat (10 g Mono, 2 g Poly, 8 g Sat); 55 mg Cholesterol; 23 g Carbohydrate (4 g Fibre, 8 g Sugar); 20 g Protein; 1000 mg Sodium

Tex-Mex Taco Soup

This slow cooker soup is a fiesta of flavour! Garnish individual servings with your favourite Tex-Mex toppings, such as broken corn chips or tortilla strips, sour cream or Monterey Jack cheese.

Cooking oil	2 tsp.	10 mL
Lean ground beef	1 lb.	454 g
Prepared beef broth	6 cups	1.5 L
Can of black beans (19 oz., 540 mL), rinsed and drained	1	1
Chopped red onion	2 cups	500 mL
Can of diced tomatoes (14 oz., 398 mL), with juice	1	1
Chopped celery	1 1/2 cups	375 mL
Grated carrot	1 1/2 cups	375 mL
Chopped red pepper	1 cup	250 mL
Chunky salsa	1 cup	250 mL
Brown sugar, packed	1 tsp.	5 mL
Dried basil	1 tsp.	5 mL
Chopped fresh cilantro (or parsley)	1 tbsp.	15 mL
Chopped green onion	2 tbsp.	30 mL

Heat cooking oil in a large frying pan on medium. Add beef and scramble-fry for about 10 minutes until no longer pink. Drain well. Transfer to a 5 to 7 quart (5 to 7 L) slow cooker.

Stir in next 10 ingredients. Cook, covered, on Low for 8 to 10 hours or on High for 4 to 5 hours until vegetables are tender.

Stir in cilantro and green onion. Makes about 14 cups (3.5 L).

1 cup (250 mL): 180 Calories; 8 g Total Fat (3.5 g Mono, .5 g Poly, 3.5 g Sat); 25 mg Cholesterol; 14 g Carbohydrate (4 g Fibre, 5 g Sugar); 11 g Protein; 610 mg Sodium

Vegetable Beef Tortellini Bowl

Beef-stuffed tortellini, Italian sausage and a variety of vegetables turn this soup into a satisfying meal.

Sliced Italian sausage	1 cup	250 mL
Chopped onion	2 cups	500 mL
Garlic cloves, minced (or 1/2 tsp., 2 mL, powder)	2	2
Prepared chicken broth	12 cups	3 L
Can of diced tomatoes (14 oz., 398 mL), drained	1	1
Grated carrot	1 1/2 cups	375 mL
Chopped zucchini (with peel)	1 1/2 cups	375 mL
Chopped yellow or red pepper	1 cup	250 mL
Bay leaves	2	2
Dried rosemary, crushed	1 tsp.	5 mL
Salt	1/4 tsp.	1 mL
Package of fresh beef-filled tortellini (12 1/2 oz., 350 g)	1	1
Chopped fresh spinach leaves, lightly packed	3 cups	750 mL

Cook Italian sausage, onion and garlic in a Dutch oven or large pot on medium-high for 5 to 10 minutes, stirring often, until onion is softened.

Stir in next 8 ingredients and bring to a boil.

Stir in tortellini and reduce heat to medium. Boil gently, uncovered, for about 8 minutes, stirring occasionally, until tortellini is tender but firm.

Stir in spinach. Cook for about 2 minutes until spinach is wilted. Remove and discard bay leaves. Makes about 15 cups (3.75 L).

1 cup (250 mL): 140 Calories; 6 g Total Fat (2 g Mono, 1 g Poly, 2 g Sat); 15 mg Cholesterol; 16 g Carbohydrate (2 g Fibre, 4 g Sugar); 5 g Protein; 730 mg Sodium

Beef and Cabbage Soup

Earthy mushrooms lend even more appeal to this one-dish meal of anise-scented broth with tender meat, bean thread noodles, tender-crisp greens and sweet carrots.

Cooking oil	1 tbsp.	15 mL
Boneless beef cross-rib roast, cut into 1 1/2 inch (3.8 cm) cubes	1 1/2 lbs.	680 g
Chopped green onion (2 inch, 5 cm, pieces)	1 1/2 cups	375 mL
Sliced fresh shiitake mushrooms	1 cup	250 mL
Thinly sliced carrot	1 cup	250 mL
Garlic cloves, sliced	3	3
Chinese rice wine	1/2 cup	125 mL
Prepared beef broth	4 cups	1 L
Soy sauce	1/4 cup	60 mL
Star anise	2	2
Cinnamon stick (4 inches, 10 cm)	1	1
Piece of ginger root (2 inch, 5 cm, length)	1	1
Salt	1 tsp.	5 mL
Bean thread noodles	4 oz.	113 g
Cornstarch	2 tbsp.	30 mL
Water	2 tbsp.	30 mL
Baby bok choy, halved lengthwise	6	6

Heat cooking oil in a large frying pan on medium-high. Add beef and cook, stirring often, until browned. Transfer with a slotted spoon to a 3 1/2 to 4 quart (3 1/2 to 4 L) slow cooker.

Add next 4 ingredients to pan and stir-fry for 2 minutes until browned.

Add rice wine and stir for 1 minute, scraping any brown bits from bottom of pan. Transfer vegetables to slow cooker.

Stir in next 6 ingredients. Cook, covered, on Low for 8 to 10 hours or on High for 4 to 5 hours. Discard star anise, cinnamon stick and ginger root. Skim and discard any fat (see Tip, page 16).

Put noodles into a bowl and cover with hot water. Let stand for 10 minutes until softened. Drain.

Stir cornstarch into water in a small cup until smooth. Add noodles, cornstarch mixture and bok choy to slow cooker and stir. Cook on High, covered, for 20 minutes until slightly thickened. Makes about 11 1/2 cups (2.9 L).

1 cup (250 mL): 130 Calories; 6 g Total Fat (2 g Mono, 1 g Poly, 1.5 g Sat); 40 mg Cholesterol; 3 g Carbohydrate (0 g Fibre, 1 g Sugar); 16 g Protein; 580 mg Sodium

Thai-style Pork Soup

Spicy curry heats up this hearty soup. You can adjust the level of spice by using more or less red curry paste.

Cooking oil	1 tbsp.	15 mL
Pork tenderloin, trimmed of fat and cut into thin strips (see Tip, below)	1/2 lb.	225 g
Thai red curry paste	1 tbsp.	15 mL
Low-sodium prepared chicken broth	4 cups	1 L
Can of cut baby corn (14 oz., 398 mL), drained	1	1
Thinly sliced red pepper	1 cup	250 mL
Fish sauce	1 tsp.	5 mL
Brown sugar, packed	1 tsp.	5 mL
Fresh spinach, stems removed, lightly packed	2 cups	500 mL
Finely shredded fresh basil	2 tbsp.	30 mL
Lime juice	1 tbsp.	15 mL

Heat cooking oil in a large pot or Dutch oven on medium-high. Add pork and cook for about 5 minutes, stirring occasionally, until browned. Transfer to a small bowl. Cover to keep warm.

Add curry paste to same large pot and cook, stirring, for about 1 minute until fragrant. Stir in next 5 ingredients and bring to a boil on medium-high. Reduce heat to medium-low. Simmer, covered, for about 5 minutes until red pepper is softened.

Stir in pork and spinach. Simmer for about 2 minutes, stirring occasionally, until pork is heated through and spinach is wilted. Stir in basil and lime juice. Makes 4 servings.

1 serving: 170 Calories; 7 g Total Fat (2.5 g Mono, 2.5 g Poly, 1 g Sat); 35 mg Cholesterol; 10 g Carbohydrate (3 g Fibre, 5 g Sugar); 18 g Protein; 1220 mg Sodium

Tip: To slice meat easily, freeze it for about 30 minutes. If you are using frozen meat, partially thaw it before slicing.

Portuguese Chowder

This robust chowder is loaded with hot sausage and vegetables in a rich, red broth. Serve with bread or buns to make a complete meal. Ham replaces the more traditional salt cod in this recipe.

Hot sausage (such as chorizo or hot Italian)	1/2 lb.	225 g
Chopped onion	1 cup	250 mL
Garlic cloves, minced (or 1/2 tsp., 2 mL, powder)	2	2
Olive (or cooking) oil	1 tbsp.	15 mL
Can of diced tomatoes (28 oz., 796 mL), with juice	1	1
Diced potato	2 cups	500 mL
Diced celery	1 cup	250 mL
Diced carrot	1 cup	250 mL
Prepared beef broth	3 cups	750 mL
Finely chopped cabbage	2 cups	500 mL
Diced cooked ham	1 cup	250 mL
Can of kidney beans (14 oz., 398 mL), drained	1	1
Dry red (or alcohol-free) wine (optional)	1/2 cup	125 mL

Remove sausage meat from casing. Scramble-fry sausage, onion and garlic in olive oil in a large pot or Dutch oven until sausage is no longer pink and onion is soft.

Add next 5 ingredients and bring to a boil. Reduce heat and simmer, covered, for 20 minutes until vegetables are cooked.

Add cabbage, ham and kidney beans. Simmer, covered, for 15 minutes until cabbage is tender.

Stir in red wine. Makes 12 cups (3 L).

1 cup (250 mL): 190 Calories; 8 g Total Fat (1.5 g Mono, 0 g Poly, 2.5 g Sat); 20 mg Cholesterol; 17 g Carbohydrate (4 g Fibre, 5 g Sugar); 10 g Protein; 690 mg Sodium

Pasta e Fagioli

Meaning "pasta and beans," pasta e fagioli is an Italian soup that has many variations, depending on what region of Italy the recipe comes from. The soup started off as peasant food, and along with the requisite pasta and beans, the cook would throw in whatever ingredients were on hand. Some versions are meatless, whereas others, like this recipe, add meat such as bacon, pancetta or sausage.

Italian sausage, casings removed, crumbled	1/2 lb.	225 g
Chopped onion	1 cup	250 mL
Sliced celery	1 cup	250 mL
Sliced carrot	1 cup	250 mL
Dried oregano	1 tsp.	5 mL
Dried basil	1 tsp.	5 mL
Garlic cloves, minced (or 1/2 tsp., 2 mL, powder)	2	2
Pepper	1/2 tsp.	2 mL
Can of white kidney beans (19 oz., 540 mL), rinsed and drained	1	1
Can of diced tomatoes (28 oz., 796 mL), with juice	1	1
Prepared chicken broth	3 cups	750 mL
Water	1 cup	250 mL
Tomato paste (see Tip, page 18)	1/4 cup	60 mL
Bay leaves	2	2
Tubetti (or other very small pasta)	1 cup	250 mL
Grated Parmesan cheese	1/4 cup	60 mL

Scramble-fry sausage in a medium frying pan on medium until no longer pink. Transfer to a 4 to 5 quart (4 to 5 L) slow cooker using a slotted spoon. Drain and discard all but 2 tsp. (10 mL) drippings.

Add next 7 ingredients to frying pan and cook for 5 to 10 minutes, stirring often, until onion is softened. Add to slow cooker.

Mash 1 cup (250 mL) kidney beans with a fork and add to slow cooker. Add remaining kidney beans to slow cooker.

Stir in next 5 ingredients. Cook, covered, on Low for 7 to 8 hours or on High for 3 1/2 to 4 hours until vegetables are tender. Remove and discard bay leaves.

Cook pasta in boiling salted water in a large uncovered saucepan for 10 to 12 minutes, stirring occasionally, until tender but firm. Drain and add to slow cooker.

Sprinkle individual servings with cheese. Makes about 12 cups (3 L).

1 cup (250 mL): 200 Calories; 9 g Total Fat (4 g Mono, 1 g Poly, 3 g Sat); 15 mg Cholesterol; 21 g Carbohydrate (5 g Fibre, 5 g Sugar); 8 g Protein; 630 mg Sodium

Kale, Bean and Bacon Soup

Serve up a pot of this delicious bean and bacon soup, the classic flavour combination updated with plenty of root vegetables and nutritious kale. This soup freezes well and can be made ahead and stored in an airtight container in the freezer for up to three months.

Bacon slices, chopped	4	4
Sliced leek (white part only)	2 cups	500 mL
Diced carrot	1 1/2 cups	375 mL
Diced celery root	1 cup	250 mL
Garlic cloves, minced	2	2
Pepper	1/2 tsp.	2 mL
Bay leaf	1	1
Prepared chicken broth	6 cups	1.5 L
Chopped kale leaves, lightly packed	3 cups	750 mL
Water	2 cups	500 mL
Can of white kidney beans (19 oz., 540 mL), rinsed and drained	1	1

Cook bacon in a large frying pan on medium until crisp. Transfer with a slotted spoon to a plate lined with paper towel to drain. Set aside. Drain and discard all but 1 tbsp. (15 mL) drippings.

Add next 6 ingredients to frying pan. Cook for about 10 minutes, stirring often, until carrot and celery root are softened. Transfer to a 5 to 7 quart (5 to 7 L) slow cooker.

Stir in next 3 ingredients. Cook, covered, on Low for 8 to 10 hours or on High for 4 to 5 hours.

Mash 2/3 cup (150 mL) beans with a fork. Add to slow cooker. Stir in remaining beans and bacon. Cook, covered, on High for about 30 minutes until heated through. Remove and discard bay leaf. Makes about 10 1/2 cups (2.6 L).

1 cup (250 mL): 150 Calories; 7 g Total Fat (3 g Mono, 1 g Poly, 2 g Sat); 10 mg Cholesterol; 16 g Carbohydrate (5 g Fibre, 3 g Sugar); 6 g Protein; 550 mg Sodium

Hearty Winter Soup

Put those harvest veggies to good use and warm up with this chunky tomato soup, thick with beans and bacon.

Bacon slices, cooked crisp and crumbled	8	8
Prepared chicken broth	6 cups	1.5 L
Chopped yellow turnip	3 cups	750 mL
Can of white kidney beans (19 oz., 540 mL), rinsed and drained	1	1
Chopped onion	1 cup	250 mL
Chopped carrot	1 cup	250 mL
Chopped celery	1/2 cup	125 mL
Tomato paste (see Tip, page 18)	1/4 cup	60 mL
Salt	1/4 tsp.	1 mL
Pepper	1/4 tsp.	1 mL
Frozen peas	1 cup	250 mL
Sprigs of fresh rosemary	2	2
Chopped fresh parsley (or 1 1/2 tsp., 7 mL, flakes)	2 tbsp.	30 mL
Lemon juice	1 tbsp.	15 mL

Combine first 10 ingredients in a 5 to 7 quart (5 to 7 L) slow cooker. Cook, covered, on Low for 9 to 10 hours or on High for 4 1/2 to 5 hours.

Add remaining 4 ingredients. Stir well. Cook, covered, on High for about 10 minutes until peas are heated through. Remove and discard rosemary sprigs. Makes about 11 cups (2.75 L).

1 cup (250 mL): 110 Calories; 2.5 g Total Fat (1 g Mono, 0 g Poly, 1 g Sat); 5 mg Cholesterol; 16 g Carbohydrate (6 g Fibre, 4 g Sugar); 6 g Protein; 530 mg Sodium

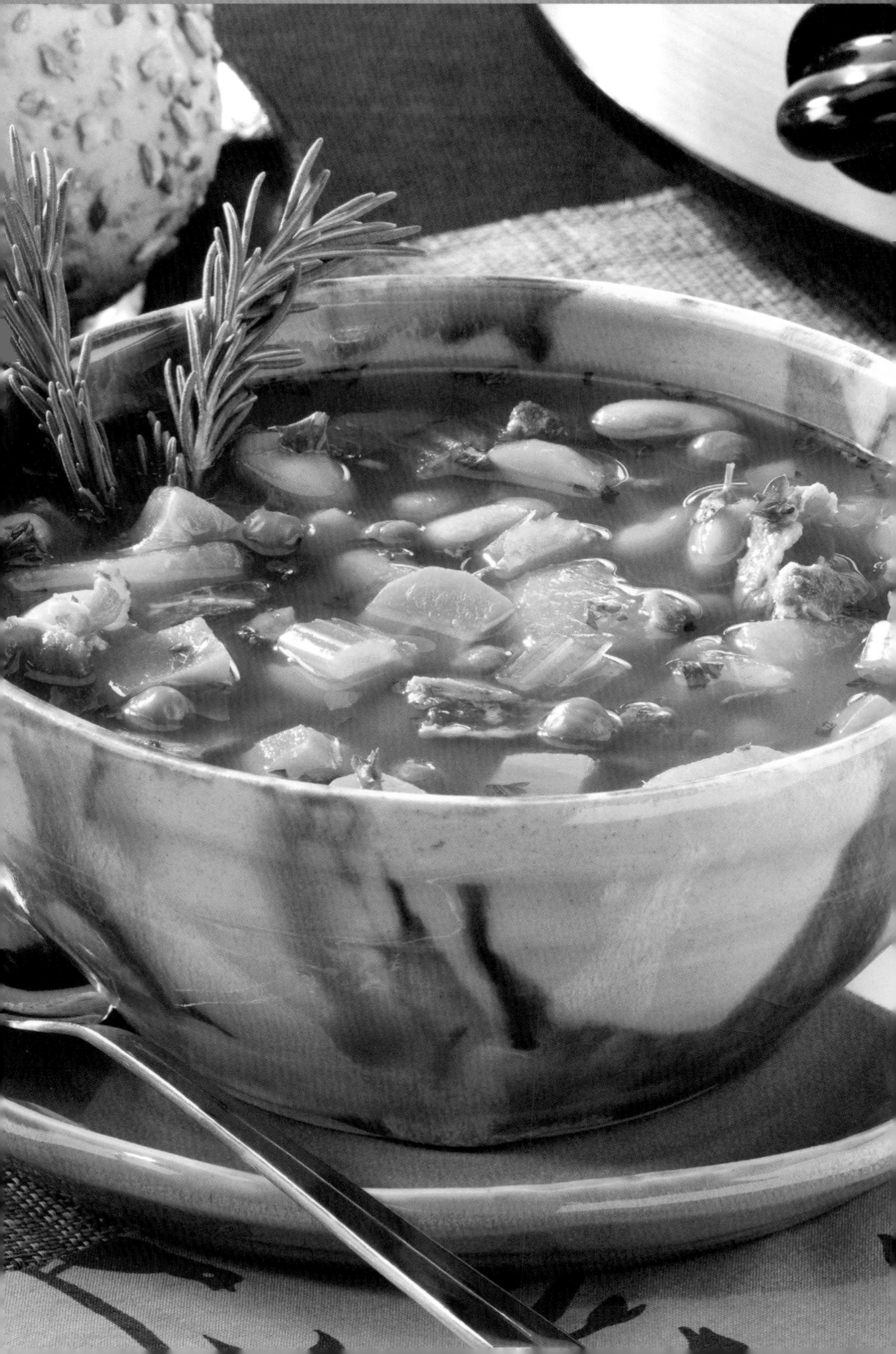

Sausage-fry Soup

The spicy sausage melds perfectly with the cabbage-like flavour of kale.

Cooking oil	1 tbsp.	15 mL
Hot Italian sausage, casings removed, chopped	1 lb.	454 g
Chopped onion	1 1/2 cups	375 mL
Garlic clove, minced (or 1/4 tsp., 1 mL, powder)	1	1
Chopped unpeeled potatoes	2 lbs.	900 g
Balsamic vinegar	3 tbsp.	45 mL
Dried rosemary, crushed	1/2 tsp.	2 mL
Salt	1/2 tsp.	2 mL
Pepper	1/4 tsp.	1 mL
Bay leaf	1	1
Prepared chicken broth	8 cups	2 L
Chopped kale leaves, lightly packed	3 cups	750 mL

Heat cooking oil in a Dutch oven or large pot on medium. Add next 3 ingredients. Scramble-fry for about 15 minutes until onion is softened and sausage is browned. Drain.

Add next 6 ingredients. Cook, stirring, for 2 minutes, scraping any brown bits from bottom of pot.

Stir in broth and bring to a boil. Reduce heat to medium-low. Simmer, covered, for 15 to 20 minutes, stirring occasionally, until potato is tender. Remove and discard bay leaf.

Stir in kale. Cook for about 5 minutes until kale is softened. Makes about 13 cups (3.25 L).

1 cup (250 mL): 210 Calories; 11 g Total Fat (0 g Mono, .5 g Poly, 4 g Sat); 25 mg Cholesterol; 18 g Carbohydrate (1 g Fibre, 2 g Sugar); 8 g Protein; 760 mg Sodium

Mexican Bean Soup

This spicy bean and rice soup is delicious on its own, but it is spectacular topped with a dollop of Jalapeño Lime Yogurt (see sidebar, page 45). If you want a more substantial soup, add in about 1/2 cup (125 mL) uncooked long grain white rice.

Cooking oil	1 tbsp.	15 mL
Chorizo sausage, casing removed, chopped	1	1
Chopped red onion	3/4 cup	175 mL
Diced red pepper	3/4 cup	175 mL
Diced carrot	1/2 cup	125 mL
Garlic clove, minced (or 1/4 tsp., 1 mL, powder)	1	1
Pepper	1/4 tsp.	1 mL
Can of kidney beans (19 oz., 540 mL), rinsed and drained	1	1
Prepared chicken broth	5 cups	1.25 L
Can of diced tomatoes (14 oz., 398 mL), with juice	1	1
Kernel corn	1 cup	250 mL
Chunky salsa	1/2 cup	125 mL
Chili powder	2 tsp.	10 mL
Bay leaf	1	1
Dried oregano	1 tsp.	5 mL
Ground cinnamon	1/2 tsp.	2 mL

Heat cooking oil in a Dutch oven or large pot on medium. Add next 6 ingredients. Cook for 5 to 10 minutes, stirring occasionally, until onion is softened. Drain.

Mash half of beans with a fork. Add to vegetable mixture.

Stir in next 8 ingredients and remaining beans and bring to a boil. Reduce heat to medium-low. Simmer, covered, for about 20 minutes, stirring occasionally. Remove and discard bay leaf. Makes about 11 cups (2.75 L).

1 cup (250 mL): 190 Calories; 6 g Total Fat (1 g Mono, 1 g Poly, 1.5 g Sat); 5 mg Cholesterol; 28 g Carbohydrate (4 g Fibre, 6 g Sugar); 7 g Protein; 830 mg Sodium

To make jalapeño lime yogurt, combine 1/2 cup (125 mL) plain yogurt, 2 tbsp. (30 mL) chopped pickled jalapeño peppers and 1 tsp. (5 mL) grated lime zest in a small cup. Makes about 2/3 cup (150 mL) yogurt. Drizzle onto individual servings.

Ham Hock and Vegetable Soup

Is there anything more inviting than a rich, smoky flavoured pea soup? Serve with warm crusty bread rolls for a complete meal.

Cooking oil	2 tbsp.	30 mL
Finely chopped onion	1 1/2 cups	375 mL
Finely chopped carrot	1 cup	250 mL
Finely chopped yellow turnip	1 cup	250 mL
Finely chopped celery	1/2 cup	125 mL
Garlic cloves, minced (or 1 tsp., 5 mL, powder)	4	4
Prepared chicken broth	8 cups	2 L
Smoked ham hocks	2 1/4 lbs.	1 kg
Can of diced tomatoes (28 oz., 796 mL), with juice	1	1
Yellow split peas, rinsed and drained	3/4 cup	175 mL
Dry red (or alcohol-free) wine	1/3 cup	75 mL
Bay leaves	2	2

Diced ham, for garnish
Chopped fresh parsley, for garnish

Heat cooking oil in a large pot or Dutch oven on medium. Stir in next 5 ingredients. Cook for about 10 minutes, stirring often, until onion is softened.

Stir in next 6 ingredients and bring to a boil. Reduce heat to medium-low. Simmer, covered, for 2 hours. Set aside to cool. Remove meat from bones. Discard bones. Chop meat and return to soup. Cover and chill in refrigerator overnight. Skim off and discard fat from surface. Reheat on medium for 10 to 15 minutes, stirring occasionally, until hot. Remove and discard bay leaves.

Garnish individual servings with diced ham and parsley. Makes about 12 1/2 cups (3.1 L).

1 cup (250 mL): 290 Calories; 20 g Total Fat (9 g Mono, 2.5 g Poly, 7 g Sat); 55 mg Cholesterol; 12 g Carbohydrate (3 g Fibre, 5 g Sugar); 16 g Protein; 570 mg Sodium

Spicy Lentil Soup

The bacon, chorizo and jalapeños give this soup a nice spicy kick with mild smoky undertones. Loaded with vegetables and lentils, this filling soup is a meal in itself.

Diced bacon (or salt pork)	1/2 cup	125 mL
Sliced chorizo (or hot Italian) sausage	8 oz.	225 g
Chopped onion	1 cup	250 mL
Garlic cloves, minced (or 1/2 tsp., 2 mL, powder)	2	2
Medium carrot, diced	1	1
Celery rib, diced	1	1
Can of roma (plum) tomatoes (28 oz., 796 mL), with juice, coarsely chopped	1	1
Can of lentils (19 oz., 540 ml), rinsed and drained	1	1
Prepared chicken broth	3 cups	750 mL
Brown sugar, packed	1 tbsp.	15 mL
Diced pickled jalapeño pepper (or other hot pepper)	1 tbsp.	15 mL
Lime juice	2 tsp.	10 mL
Ground cumin	1 tsp.	5 mL
Ground coriander	1/2 tsp.	2 mL
Chopped fresh parsley (or cilantro), for garnish		

Cook bacon in a large pot or Dutch oven on medium for about 3 minutes until starting to brown. Add sausage and cook, stirring, until browned. Drain and discard all but 2 tsp. (10 mL) drippings from pot.

Add next 4 ingredients. Cook for 2 minutes, stirring and scraping up any brown bits from bottom of pot. (If necessary, add 1/4 cup [60 mL] water to loosen brown bits.)

Stir in next 8 ingredients and bring to a boil. Reduce heat to medium-low. Simmer, covered, for 20 to 30 minutes until carrot is tender.

Sprinkle individual servings with parsley. Makes 9 cups (2.25 L).

1 cup (250 mL): 260 Calories; 14 g Total Fat (3 g Mono, .5 g Poly, 4.5 g Sat); 25 mg Cholesterol; 21 g Carbohydrate (4 g Fibre, 6 g Sugar); 11 g Protein; 800 mg Sodium

Quick Leftover Pork Soup

A delicious reincarnation for leftover pork—just toss it into this hearty soup for a warm, filling meal.

Cooking oil	2 tsp.	10 mL
Chopped onion	1 1/2 cups	375 mL
Dry white (or alcohol-free) wine (optional)	1/4 cup	60 mL
Prepared vegetable broth	4 cups	1 L
Canned white kidney beans	1 cup	250 mL
Canned red kidney beans	1 cup	250 mL
Can of Italian-style diced tomatoes (14 oz., 398 mL), with juice	1	1
Diced leftover roast pork	2 cups	500 mL
Diced potato	2 cups	500 mL
Pepper	1/2 tsp.	2 mL
Frozen peas	3/4 cup	175 mL
Chopped fresh basil (or 1 1/2 tsp., 7 mL, dried)	2 tbsp.	30 mL

Heat cooking oil in a large pot or Dutch oven on medium. Add onion and cook for 5 to 10 minutes, stirring often, until softened.

Add wine. Bring to a boil and boil for 1 minute.

Stir in next 7 ingredients and bring to a boil. Reduce heat to medium-low. Simmer, covered, for about 45 minutes until potato is soft.

Add peas. Heat, stirring, for 3 to 5 minutes until peas are tender. Stir in basil. Makes 9 cups (2.25 L).

1 cup (250 mL): 180 Calories; 6 g Total Fat (0 g Mono, .5 g Poly, 6 g Sat); 25 mg Cholesterol; 18 g Carbohydrate (5 g Fibre, 5 g Sugar); 12 g Protein; 880 mg Sodium

Ham and Cheese Chowder

The favourite flavour combination of ham and cheese in a soup! This kid-friendly chowder is simple to prepare and has a quick cooking time—perfect for lunch or after school. Garnish with grated Cheddar cheese for an attractive presentation.

Butter (or hard margarine)	2 tbsp.	30 mL
Chopped onion	1 cup	250 mL
All-purpose flour	2 tbsp.	30 mL
Dill weed	1/2 tsp.	2 mL
Pepper	1/4 tsp.	1 mL
Prepared chicken broth	2 cups	500 mL
Diced peeled potato	2 cups	500 mL
Grated medium Cheddar cheese	2 cups	500 mL
Milk	1 cup	250 mL
Diced cooked ham	1 cup	250 mL

Grated Cheddar cheese, for garnish

Melt butter in a large saucepan on medium. Add onion and cook for 5 to 10 minutes, stirring often, until softened.

Add next 3 ingredients. Cook, stirring, for 1 minute.

Slowly stir in broth until combined. Cook, stirring, until boiling and thickened.

Stir in potato and bring to a boil. Reduce heat to medium-low. Simmer, partially covered, for 15 to 20 minutes, stirring occasionally, until potato is tender.

Add next 3 ingredients. Cook, stirring, for about 5 minutes until heated through.

Garnish individual servings with grated Cheddar cheese. Makes about 5 cups (1.25 L).

1 cup (250 mL): *550 Calories; 36 g Total Fat (2.5 g Mono, .5 g Poly, 23 g Sat); 125 mg Cholesterol; 24 g Carbohydrate (2 g Fibre, 5 g Sugar); 33 g Protein; 1140 mg Sodium*

Two Potato Chowder

Garlic sausage and rustic potatoes combine in this comforting, old-fashioned chowder.

Chopped garlic sausage	1/2 cup	125 mL
Chopped onion	1 cup	250 mL
Diced celery	1 cup	250 mL
All-purpose flour	2 tbsp.	30 mL
Prepared chicken broth	4 cups	1 L
Diced, peeled sweet potato (or yam)	1 1/2 cups	375 mL
Diced, peeled red potato	1 1/2 cups	375 mL
Dried rosemary, crushed	1/4 tsp.	1 mL
Ground thyme	1/4 tsp.	1 mL
Pepper	1/4 tsp.	1 mL
Milk	1 cup	250 mL

Cook garlic sausage, onion and celery in a large saucepan on medium for 5 to 10 minutes, stirring often, until onion is softened.

Sprinkle with flour and cook, stirring, for 1 minute.

Slowly add 1 cup (250 mL) broth. Cook, stirring, until boiling and thickened. Stir in remaining broth and bring to a boil.

Stir in next 5 ingredients and reduce heat to medium-low. Simmer, partially covered, for 15 to 20 minutes, stirring occasionally, until potato is tender.

Add milk. Cook, stirring, for 1 to 2 minutes until heated through. Makes about 8 cups (2 L).

1 cup (250 mL): 220 Calories; 13 g Total Fat (6 g Mono, 1.5 g Poly, 4.5 g Sat); 20 mg Cholesterol; 18 g Carbohydrate (2 g Fibre, 5 g Sugar); 6 g Protein; 570 mg Sodium

Barley and Lamb Soup

There's plenty of garden goodness in this rich lamb and barley soup, with a double dose of flavour from beer and pearl barley! This tasty soup can be stored in an airtight container in the freezer for up to three months.

Cooking oil	2 tsp.	10 mL
Lean ground lamb	1/2 lb.	225 g
Chopped onion	1 cup	250 mL
Sliced leek (white part only)	1 cup	250 mL
Diced celery	1/2 cup	125 mL
Dark beer (such as honey brown)	1 1/2 cups	375 mL
Prepared beef broth	6 cups	1.5 L
Water	2 cups	500 mL
Diced carrot	1 cup	250 mL
Diced parsnip	1 cup	250 mL
Diced yellow turnip (rutabaga)	1 cup	250 mL
Pearl barley	1/2 cup	125 mL
Tomato paste (see Tip, page 18)	1 tbsp.	15 mL
Dried rosemary, crushed	1/2 tsp.	2 mL
Dried thyme	1/2 tsp.	2 mL
Salt	3/4 tsp.	4 mL
Pepper	1/2 tsp.	2 mL
Bay leaf	1	1
Diced zucchini (with peel)	1 cup	250 mL

Heat cooking oil in a Dutch oven on medium-high. Add next 4 ingredients. Scramble-fry for about 5 minutes until lamb is no longer pink.

Add beer and cook, stirring and scraping any brown bits from bottom of pan, until boiling.

Stir in next 12 ingredients and bring to a boil. Reduce heat to medium-low. Simmer, covered, for about 45 minutes until barley is tender.

Stir in zucchini. Simmer, covered, for about 10 minutes until zucchini is tender. Skim and discard fat (see Tip, page 16). Remove and discard bay leaf. Makes about 12 1/2 cups (3.1 L).

1 cup (250 mL): 130 Calories; 4 g Total Fat (0 g Mono, .5 g Poly, 1.5 g Sat); 15 mg Cholesterol; 16 g Carbohydrate (3 g Fibre, 4 g Sugar); 6 g Protein; 520 mg Sodium

Lamb Bouquet Soup

Some people are intimidated by the thought of cooking lamb shanks, but they needn't be. The long cooking time and low temperature of your slow cooker ensure the lamb in this flavourful soup is tender and juicy, a perfect complement to the white beans and potato.

Dried white beans	1 cup	250 mL
Prepared beef (or chicken) broth	7 cups	1.75 L
Lamb shanks (about 1 1/2 lbs., 680 g)	2	2
Chopped onion	1 cup	250 mL
Chopped celery	1 cup	250 mL
Diced peeled potato	1/2 cup	125 mL
Sliced carrot	1/2 cup	125 mL
Chopped fresh rosemary (or 1/2 tsp., 2 mL, dried, crushed)	2 tsp.	10 mL
Paprika	1/2 tsp.	2 mL
Bay leaves	2	2
Whole allspice	2	2
Sprigs of fresh parsley	2	2
Whole black peppercorns	8	8
Garlic clove	1	1
Brown sugar, packed	2 tbsp.	30 mL
Grated lemon zest	1 tsp.	5 mL
Salt	1/2 tsp.	2 mL

Measure beans into a small heatproof bowl. Add boiling water until 2 inches (5 cm) above beans. Let stand for at least 1 hour until cool. Drain and rinse beans. Transfer to a 5 to 7 quart (5 to 7 L) slow cooker.

Stir in next 8 ingredients.

Place next 5 ingredients on a 10 inch (25 cm) square piece of cheesecloth. Draw up corners and tie with butcher's string to form a bouquet garni. Submerge in liquid in slow cooker. Cook, covered, on Low for about 10 hours or on High for about 5 hours until beans are tender and lamb is falling off bones. Remove and discard bouquet garni. Transfer shanks to a cutting board using a slotted spoon. Keep bean mixture covered. Remove lamb from bones. Discard bones. Chop lamb coarsely and return to slow cooker.

Stir in remaining 3 ingredients. Cook, covered, on High for about 15 minutes until heated through. Makes about 11 cups (2.75 L).

1 cup (250 mL): 140 Calories; 3 g Total Fat (1 g Mono, 0 g Poly, 1 g Sat); 35 mg Cholesterol; 14 g Carbohydrate (3 g Fibre, 5 g Sugar); 14 g Protein; 650 mg Sodium

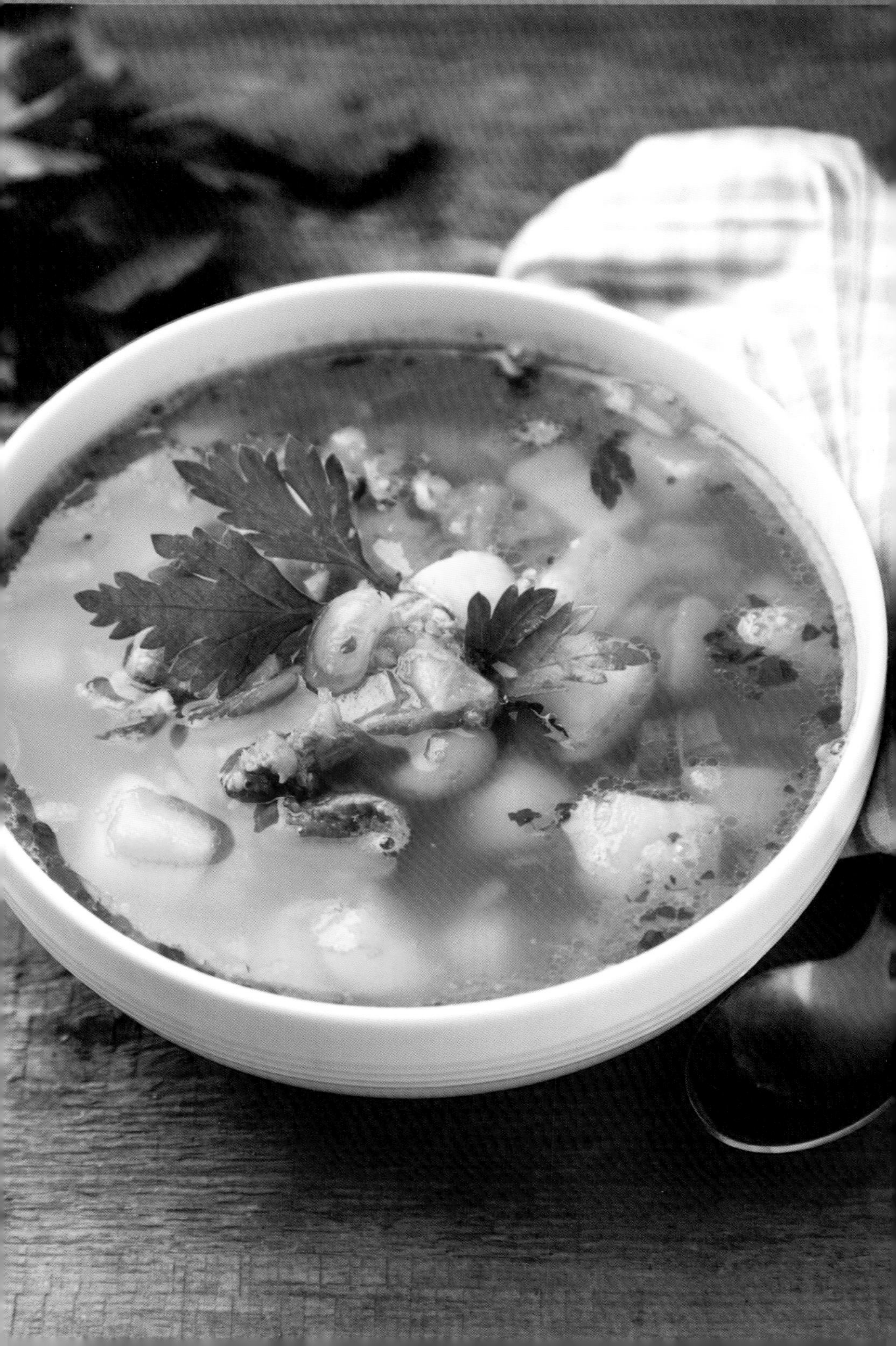

Comfort Chicken Noodle Soup

Nothing evokes the comfort of home like a piping hot bowl of chicken noodle soup, especially when it is made from scratch. We've used spaghetti noodles in this recipe, but feel free to substitute egg noodles, if you prefer.

Bone-in chicken parts (see Tip, page 61)	4 lbs.	1.8 kg
Water	10 cups	2.5 L
Celery ribs, with leaves, halved	2	2
Large onion, quartered	1	1
Large carrot, halved	1	1
Sprigs of fresh thyme	3	3
Sprig of fresh parsley	1	1
Bay leaves	2	2
Garlic clove	1	1
Whole black peppercorns	12	12
Cooking oil	2 tsp.	10 mL
Chopped onion	1/2 cup	125 mL
Chopped carrot	1/2 cup	125 mL
Chopped celery	1/2 cup	125 mL
Spaghetti, broken into about 3 inch (7.5 cm) pieces	3 oz.	85 g
Chopped fresh parsley	1/4 cup	60 mL
Salt	3/4 tsp.	4 mL
Pepper	1/4 tsp.	1 mL

For the stock, put chicken and water into a Dutch oven or large pot and bring to a boil. Boil, uncovered, for 5 minutes without stirring. Skim and discard foam from side of pot.

Stir in next 8 ingredients and bring to a boil. Reduce heat to medium-low. Simmer, uncovered, for about 3 hours, stirring occasionally, until chicken is tender and starts to fall off bones. Remove from heat. Transfer chicken and bones to a cutting board using slotted spoon. Remove chicken from bones. Discard bones. Chop enough chicken to make 2 cups (500 mL). Reserve remaining chicken for another use. Strain stock through a sieve into a large bowl. Discard solids. Skim fat from stock (see Tip, page 16).

For the soup, heat cooking oil in a large saucepan on medium. Add next 3 ingredients. Cook for 5 to 10 minutes, stirring often, until onion is softened. Add stock and bring to a boil.

Add spaghetti and cook, uncovered, for about 10 minutes, stirring occasionally, until spaghetti and vegetables are tender.

Add chicken and remaining 3 ingredients. Cook, stirring, until chicken is heated through. Makes about 7 1/2 cups (1.9 L).

1 cup (250 mL): 120 Calories; 2.5 g Total Fat (1 g Mono, 1 g Poly, 0 g Sat); 25 mg Cholesterol; 14 g Carbohydrate (2 g Fibre, 3 g Sugar); 9 g Protein; 310 mg Sodium

Tip: Use whichever cuts of chicken you prefer as long as the weight used is equal to that listed.

Chicken Corn Soup

Your standard chicken soup has been given a Mexican makeover with the addition of chipotle, lime and cilantro.

Canola oil	1 tsp.	5 mL
Kernel corn	2 cups	500 mL
Chopped onion	1 cup	250 mL
Garlic cloves, minced	2	2
(or 1/2 tsp., 2 mL, powder)		
Finely chopped chipotle peppers in adobo sauce (see Tip, page 120)	1/2 tsp.	2 mL
Low-sodium prepared chicken broth	3 cups	750 mL
Can of diced tomatoes (14 oz., 398 mL), with juice	1	1
Pepper	1/4 tsp.	1 mL
Chopped cooked chicken (see Tip, below)	2 cups	500 mL
Chopped fresh cilantro	1 tbsp.	15 mL
Lime juice	1 tbsp.	15 mL

Heat canola oil in a large saucepan on medium-high. Add next 4 ingredients. Cook, uncovered, for about 4 minutes, stirring often, until onion is softened.

Stir in next 3 ingredients and bring to a boil. Reduce heat to medium. Boil gently, covered, for 6 minutes to blend flavours.

Add chicken. Cook, stirring, for about 3 minutes until heated through.

Stir in cilantro and lime juice. Makes 6 servings.

1 serving: 170 Calories; 7 g Total Fat (2.5 g Mono, 1 g Poly, 5 g Sat); 35 mg Cholesterol; 14 g Carbohydrate (3 g Fibre, 9 g Sugar); 13 g Protein; 840 mg Sodium

Tip: Don't have any leftover chicken or turkey? Start with 2 boneless, skinless chicken breasts (about 5 oz., 140 g, each) or 1 boneless, skinless turkey breast (about 10 oz., 285 g). Place in a large frying pan with 1 cup (250 mL) water or chicken broth. Simmer, covered, for 12 to 14 minutes until no longer pink inside. Drain and chop. Makes about 2 cups (500 mL).

Only Chicken Soup

This creamy, golden soup is loaded with vegetables, but you can't see them because everything but the chicken is blended smooth. The perfect soup to trick your vegetable-averse kids into eating their veggies!

Chopped onion	1 cup	250 mL
Chopped celery	1 cup	250 mL
Garlic clove, minced	1	1
(or 1/4 tsp., 1 mL, powder)		
Cooking oil	1 tbsp.	15 mL
Prepared chicken broth	6 cups	1.5 L
Chopped carrot (about 2 medium)	1 cup	250 mL
Medium potatoes, peeled and cut into 8 chunks	2	2
Peeled diced zucchini	1 1/2 cups	375 mL
Boneless, skinless chicken breast halves (about 2)	8 oz.	225 g
Parsley flakes	2 tsp.	10 mL
Bay leaf	1	1

Sauté onion, celery and garlic in cooking oil in a large uncovered pot or Dutch oven until onion is soft and clear.

Stir in remaining 7 ingredients. Simmer, covered, for 1 hour. Transfer chicken to a cutting board. Remove and discard bay leaf. Following manufacturer's instructions for processing hot liquids, carefully process with a hand blender, or in a blender in batches, until smooth. Cut chicken into bite-sized pieces. Return to soup. Makes 10 2/3 cups (2.7 L).

1 cup (250 mL): 90 Calories; 1.5 g Total Fat (.5 g Mono, 1 g Poly, 0 g Sat); 10 mg Cholesterol; 12 g Carbohydrate (2 g Fibre, 3 g Sugar); 6 g Protein; 350 mg Sodium

Gingery Noodle Soup

Reminiscent of the clean, fresh flavours of Vietnamese cuisine, this chicken soup is so easy to make at home—it's less trouble than takeout! Add more chili sauce and herbs if you want your soup to have a little more kick.

Prepared chicken broth	6 cups	1.5 mL
Piece of ginger root	1	1
(2 inch, 5 cm, length)		
Fish sauce	2 tsp.	5 mL
Sweet chili sauce	2 tsp.	5 mL
Fresh bean sprouts	1 cup	250 mL
Shredded cooked chicken	1 cup	250 mL
Coarsely chopped fresh cilantro or parsley	2 tbsp.	30 mL
Lime juice	1 tsp.	5 mL
Thin rice stick noodles	4 oz.	113 g

Combine first 4 ingredients in a medium saucepan and bring to a boil. Reduce heat to medium-low. Simmer for about 5 minutes until ginger is fragrant. Remove and discard ginger. Remove from heat.

Stir in next 4 ingredients. Let stand, covered, for about 5 minutes until heated through.

Put noodles into a medium bowl and cover with boiling water. Let stand for about 3 minutes until tender. Drain and divide between 4 soup bowls. Ladle soup over noodles and stir gently. Makes 4 servings.

1 serving: 250 Calories; 8 g Total Fat (0 g Mono, 0 g Poly, 0 g Sat); 45 mg Cholesterol; 30 g Carbohydrate (0 g Fibre, 3 g Sugar); 12 g Protein; 1110 mg Sodium

Coconut Chicken Soup

In this smooth, creamy soup, mild curry flavours pair perfectly with the sweet taste of coconut.

Peanut (or cooking) oil	1 tbsp.	15 mL
Boneless, skinless chicken breast halves (about 3)	3/4 lb.	340 g
Peanut (or cooking) oil	1 tbsp.	15 mL
Finely chopped red onion	1 cup	250 mL
Coarsely grated carrot	1/2 cup	125 mL
Finely grated peeled ginger root	1 tsp.	5 mL
Garlic cloves, minced (or 1/2 tsp., 2 mL, powder)	2	2
Curry powder	1 tbsp.	15 mL
Chili powder	1 tsp.	5 mL
Ground allspice	1/4 tsp.	1 mL
Ground nutmeg	1/4 tsp.	1 mL
Cans of coconut milk (14 oz., 398 mL, each)	2	2
Salt	1/2 tsp.	2 mL
Cooked white rice	1 cup	250 mL
Lime (or lemon) juice	1 1/2 tbsp.	25 mL

Heat first amount of peanut oil in a large pot or Dutch oven on medium. Add chicken and cook for about 3 minutes per side until browned. Remove from pot. Chop and set aside.

Heat second amount of peanut oil in same pot on medium-low. Add next 4 ingredients and cook for about 10 minutes, stirring occasionally, until onion is soft.

Add next 4 ingredients. Cook, stirring, for 1 to 2 minutes until fragrant.

Stir in coconut milk and salt and bring to a gentle boil. Reduce heat to medium-low. Simmer, uncovered, for 5 minutes to blend flavours. Add chicken, rice and lime juice. Cook, stirring, for 2 to 3 minutes until hot. Makes about 5 cups (1.25 L).

1 cup (250 mL): 450 Calories; 39 g Total Fat (3.5 g Mono, 4 g Poly, 29 g Sat); 40 mg Cholesterol; 11 g Carbohydrate (1 g Fibre, 2 g Sugar); 20 g Protein; 270 mg Sodium

Cheddar Chicken Soup

Serve this lovely orange soup with some herbed biscuits and apple slices for a well-rounded supper.

Prepared chicken broth	2 1/2 cups	625 mL
Grated carrot	3/4 cup	175 mL
Grated peeled potato	1/2 cup	125 mL
Finely diced celery	1/4 cup	60 mL
Finely diced onion	1/4 cup	60 mL
Diced cooked chicken	2 cups	500 mL
Milk	1 cup	250 mL
Steak sauce	1 tsp.	5 mL
All-purpose flour	1/4 cup	60 mL
Salt	1/2 tsp.	2 mL
Pepper	1/8 tsp.	0.5 mL
Milk	1/2 cup	125 mL
Grated sharp Cheddar cheese	2 cups	500 mL

Sour cream, for garnish
Chopped fresh chives, for garnish

Combine first 5 ingredients in a large saucepan and bring to a boil. Reduce heat to medium-low. Simmer, uncovered, for about 5 minutes until vegetables are tender.

Stir in next 3 ingredients and bring to a boil. Reduce heat to medium.

Combine next 3 ingredients in a small bowl. Stir in second amount of milk until smooth. Slowly stir into vegetable mixture until boiling and slightly thickened.

Add cheese. Cook, stirring, on medium-low until melted. Do not boil.

Garnish individual servings with sour cream and chives. Makes about 6 1/2 cups (1.6 L).

1 cup (250 mL): 290 Calories; 17 g Total Fat (3.5 g Mono, 0 g Poly, 8 g Sat); 70 mg Cholesterol; 13 g Carbohydrate (0 g Fibre, 5 g Sugar); 21 g Protein; 670 mg Sodium

Lemony Chicken Quinoa Soup

This delightful soup has all the same tangy flavours as lemon chicken but with the added nutritional benefits of quinoa.

Cooking oil	1 tbsp.	15 mL
Boneless, skinless chicken breast halves, cut in half lengthwise and cut crosswise into thin strips	3/4 lb.	340 g
Chopped onion	1 cup	250 mL
Thinly sliced carrot	1 cup	250 mL
Garlic clove	1	1
Prepared chicken broth	7 cups	1.75 mL
Quinoa	3/4 cup	175 mL cup
Grated lemon zest (see Tip, below)	1 tsp.	5 mL
Fresh spinach leaves, lightly packed, chopped	2 cups	500 mL
Lemon juice	2 tbsp.	30 mL

Heat cooking oil in a large saucepan on medium-high. Add chicken and cook for about 4 minutes, stirring often, until no longer pink. With a slotted spoon, transfer chicken to a plate.

Reduce heat to medium. Add next 3 ingredients. Cook for about 10 minutes, scraping any brown bits from the pan, until onion and carrot start to soften.

Add next 3 ingredients and chicken. Bring to a boil. Reduce heat to medium-low. Simmer, partially covered, for about 20 minutes, stirring occasionally until quinoa is tender.

Stir in spinach and lemon juice. Cook for about 5 minutes, stirring occasionally, until spinach is wilted. Makes about 9 1/2 cups (2.4 L)

1 cup (250 mL): 130 Calories; 3 g Total Fat (1 g Mono, 1.5 g Poly, 0 g Sat); 20 mg Cholesterol; 15 g Carbohydrate (2 g Fibre, 2 g Sugar); 11 g Protein; 470 mg Sodium

Tip: When a recipe calls for grated zest and juice, it's easier to grate the fruit first and then juice it. Be careful not to grate down to the pith (white part of the peel), which is bitter and is best avoided.

Asian Meatball Soup

Meatballs may be unexpected in an Asian-style soup, but they're absolutely at home in this light and delicate ginger and soy broth.

Large egg, fork-beaten	1	1
Fine dry bread crumbs	3 tbsp.	45 mL
Finely chopped water chestnut	2 tbsp.	30 mL
Soy sauce	2 tsp.	10 mL
Cornstarch	1 tsp.	5 mL
Finely grated ginger root (or 1/4 tsp., 1 mL, powder)	1 tsp.	5 mL
Salt	1/4 tsp.	1 mL
Pepper	1/4 tsp.	1 mL
Extra-lean ground chicken	6 oz.	170 g
Frozen, uncooked shrimp (peeled and deveined), thawed and finely chopped	1 oz.	28 g
Low-sodium prepared chicken broth	6 cups	1.5 L
Ginger root slices (1/4 inch, 6 mm, thick)	3	3
Glass noodles	4 oz.	113 g
Sliced carrots	1 cup	250 mL
Thinly sliced bok choy	2 cups	500 mL
Bean sprouts	1/2 cup	125 mL
Chopped green onion (optional)	1	1

For the meatballs, combine first 8 ingredients in a medium bowl. Add chicken and shrimp. Mix well. Roll into 3/4 inch (2 cm) balls.

For the soup, bring broth and ginger root slices to a boil in a large saucepan or Dutch oven. Reduce heat to medium. Add meatballs and boil gently, uncovered, for 5 minutes. Reduce heat to medium-low.

Stir in noodles and carrots. Simmer, uncovered, for about 5 minutes until noodles are almost tender.

Stir in bok choy. Simmer, uncovered, for about 2 minutes until tender-crisp.

Stir in bean sprouts and green onion. Remove and discard ginger root. Makes 6 servings.

1 serving: 150 Calories; 1.5 g Total Fat (0 g Mono, 0 g Poly, 0 g Sat); 60 mg Cholesterol; 22 g Carbohydrate (1 g Fibre, 2 g Sugar); 14 g Protein; 980 mg Sodium

Cock-a-leekie

This soup comes straight from the Highlands of Scotland to your slow cooker. And although the name seems a bit nonsensical, it's actually derived from its traditional ingredients: cock, for rooster, and leekie, for leeks.

Bacon slices, diced	4	4
Sliced leek (white part only)	4 cups	1 L
Salt	1 tsp.	5 mL
Pearl barley	1/2 cup	125 mL
Chopped celery	1/2 cup	125 mL
Bone-in chicken parts, skin removed (see Tip, page 61)	3 1/2 lb.	1.6 kg
Prepared chicken broth	7 cups	1.75 L
Whole black peppercorns	8	8
Sprigs of fresh parsley	4	4
Sprig of fresh thyme	1	1
Bay leaf	1	1

Cook bacon in a large frying pan on medium for about 5 minutes until almost crisp.

Add leek. Sprinkle with salt. Cook, stirring occasionally, for about 5 minutes until leek starts to soften. Transfer to a 5 to 7 quart (5 to 7 L) slow cooker.

Layer next 4 ingredients, in order given, over leek mixture. Add broth.

Place next 4 ingredients on a 10 inch (25 cm) square piece of cheesecloth. Draw up corners and tie with butcher's string to make a bouquet garni. Submerge in liquid in slow cooker. Cook, covered, on Low for 8 to 10 hours or on High for 4 to 5 hours. Remove and discard bouquet garni. Transfer chicken to a cutting board using a slotted spoon. Remove chicken from bones. Discard bones. Chop chicken into bite-size pieces and return to soup. Makes about 11 1/2 cups (2.9 L).

1 cup (250 mL): 300 Calories; 9 g Total Fat (4 g Mono, 1.5 g Poly, 2 g Sat); 125 mg Cholesterol; 25 g Carbohydrate (4 g Fibre, 9 g Sugar); 32 g Protein; 820 mg Sodium

A bouquet garni is a small bundle of herbs used to flavour stocks and soups. The ingredients vary depending on the dish, but the basic version is a sprig each of parsley and thyme and one bay leaf, all tied together or placed in a bag of cheesecloth for easy removal before serving.

Chipotle Chicken Fiesta

Avocado, corn chips and chipotle chicken—all the fixings for a fine fiesta. Store-bought corn chips work fine in this recipe, but we like to make our own out of corn tortillas that have been cut into strips and baked until crispy.

Cooking oil	2 tbsp.	30 mL
Boneless, skinless chicken breast halves, cut into 3/4 inch (2 cm) pieces	1/2 lb.	225 g
Chopped red onion	1 cup	250 mL
Chopped green pepper	1 cup	250 mL
Garlic cloves, minced (or 1/2 tsp., 2 mL, powder)	2	2
Prepared chicken broth	5 cups	1.25 L
Kernel corn	2 cups	500 mL
Can of diced tomatoes (14 oz., 398 mL), with juice	1	1
Dried oregano	1/2 tsp.	2 mL
Chipotle pepper in adobo sauce, chopped (see Tip, page 120)	1	1
Lime juice	2 tbsp.	30 mL
Corn chips	1 1/2 cups	375 mL
Ripe medium avocado, diced	1	1
Chopped fresh cilantro	3 tbsp.	45 mL
Grated Monterey Jack cheese (optional)	1 cup	250 mL

Heat cooking oil in a large saucepan on medium-high. Add chicken and cook for 3 to 5 minutes, stirring often, until starting to brown.

Add next 3 ingredients. Cook for 5 to 10 minutes, stirring often, until onion is softened.

Stir in next 5 ingredients and bring to a boil. Reduce heat to medium-low. Simmer, partially covered, for 15 minutes, stirring occasionally, to blend flavours.

Stir in lime juice. Sprinkle next 3 ingredients and cheese, if using, on individual servings. Makes 6 servings.

1 serving: 510 Calories; 20 g Total Fat (5 g Mono, 3.5 g Poly, 4.5 g Sat); 40 mg Cholesterol; 67 g Carbohydrate (8 g Fibre, 7 g Sugar); 22 g Protein; 1270 mg Sodium

Fall Harvest Feast

Bacon, chicken and pumpkin might seem like an odd combination, but once you try it, you'll be hooked!

Bacon slices, chopped	4	4
Boneless, skinless chicken breast halves, chopped	1 lb.	454 g
Chopped onion	1 cup	250 mL
Chopped celery	1/2 cup	125 mL
Chopped carrot	1/2 cup	125 mL
Chicken (or vegetable) broth	1/4 cup	60 mL
Chicken (or vegetable) broth	6 cups	1.5 L
Can of pure pumpkin (no spices) (14 oz., 398 mL)	1	1
Dried thyme	1/4 tsp.	1 mL
Ground sage	1/8 tsp.	0.5 mL

Cook bacon in a large saucepan on medium until crisp. Transfer with a slotted spoon to paper towels to drain. Set aside.

Heat 1 tbsp. (15 mL) drippings in same saucepan on medium-high. Add chicken and cook for about 8 minutes, stirring often, until browned.

Add next 4 ingredients. Cook, stirring, for about 5 to 10 minutes, scraping any brown bits from bottom of pan, until vegetables are softened.

Stir in remaining 4 ingredients and bring to a boil. Reduce heat to medium-low. Simmer, covered, for about 30 minutes, stirring occasionally, until vegetables are tender. Stir in bacon. Makes about 8 1/2 cups (2.1 L).

1 cup (250 mL): 180 Calories; 9 g Total Fat (4 g Mono, 1 g Poly, 3 g Sat); 45 mg Cholesterol; 9 g Carbohydrate (2 g Fibre, 4 g Sugar); 15 g Protein; 590 mg Sodium

Chicken Basil Souper

This soup, chock full of chicken and vegetables, is quick and easy to prepare.

Cooking oil	1 tbsp.	15 mL
Boneless, skinless chicken thighs, chopped	3/4 lb.	340 g
Chopped onion	1 cup	250 mL
Chopped carrot	1 cup	250 mL
All-purpose flour	2 tbsp.	30 mL
Prepared chicken broth	4 cups	1 L
Can of diced tomatoes (14 oz., 398 mL), drained	1	1
Bacon slices, cooked crisp and crumbled	4	4
Pepper	1/4 tsp.	1 mL
Chopped fresh basil	3 tbsp.	45 mL
Chopped fresh parsley	2 tbsp.	30 mL
Grated Parmesan cheese (optional)	3 tbsp.	45 mL

Heat cooking oil in a large saucepan on medium-high. Add next 3 ingredients and cook for 5 to 10 minutes, stirring often, until onion is softened.

Add flour and cook, stirring, for 1 minute.

Slowly add 1 cup (250 mL) broth. Cook, stirring, until mixture is boiling and slightly thickened. Stir in remaining broth.

Stir in next 3 ingredients and bring to a boil. Reduce heat to medium-low. Simmer, covered, for 15 to 20 minutes, stirring occasionally, until vegetables are tender.

Stir in basil and parsley. Sprinkle Parmesan cheese on individual servings, if using. Makes about 8 cups (2 L).

1 cup (250 mL): 140 Calories; 6 g Total Fat (2 g Mono, 1.5 g Poly, 1.5 g Sat); 40 mg Cholesterol; 9 g Carbohydrate (1 g Fibre, 4 g Sugar); 12 g Protein; 560 mg Sodium

Classic Turkey Soup

Don't throw out the bones once the turkey has been carved. Simmer them on the stovetop to make the stock for this delicious turkey soup.

Leftover turkey carcass	1	1
Cold water	18 cups	4.5 L
Celery ribs, with leaves, halved	6	6
Medium onion, halved	1	1
Medium carrot, halved	1	1
Garlic clove	1	1
Bay leaf	1	1
Whole black peppercorns	10	10
Water	1 1/2 cups	375 mL
Short grain white rice	1 cup	250 mL
Chopped onion	1 cup	250 mL
Chopped celery	1 cup	250 mL
Chopped carrot	1 cup	250 mL
Diced peeled potato	1 cup	250 mL
Parsley flakes	1 tbsp.	15 mL
Salt	2 tsp.	10 mL
Pepper	1/2 tsp.	2 mL
Dried thyme	1/2 tsp.	2 mL
Dried sage	1/2 tsp.	2 mL
Chopped cooked turkey	2 cups	500 mL
Half-and-half cream (optional)	1/2 cup	125 mL

For the stock, break up turkey carcass to fit in a large pot. Add first amount of water and bring to a boil. Boil, uncovered, for 5 minutes without stirring. Skim and discard foam from side of pot.

Stir in next 6 ingredients and reduce heat to medium-low. Simmer, partially covered, for about 3 hours, stirring occasionally, until turkey falls off bones. Remove from heat. Discard larger bones. Strain stock through a sieve into a separate large pot. Discard solids.

For the soup, add next 11 ingredients to stock in pot and bring to a boil. Reduce heat to medium-low. Simmer, partially covered, for about 30 minutes, stirring occasionally, until vegetables and rice are tender.

Add turkey and cream, if using. Cook for about 5 minutes, stirring occasionally, until heated through. Makes about 14 cups (3.5 L).

1 cup (250 mL): 120 Calories; 2.5 g Total Fat (1 g Mono, .5 g Poly, .5 g Sat); 15 mg Cholesterol; 18 g Carbohydrate (2 g Fibre, 2 g Sugar); 6 g Protein; 390 mg Sodium

Turkey Corn Chowder

This is not your standard corn chowder. We've kicked the flavour up more than a few notches by adding tender turkey, smoky bacon and fiery chilies.

Cooking oil	1 tbsp.	15 mL
Boneless, skinless turkey breast halves, chopped	1 lb.	454 g
Chopped onion	1 cup	250 mL
Chopped cooked bacon	3/4 cup	175 mL
Chopped celery	1/2 cup	125 mL
Dried crushed chilies	1/2 tsp.	2 mL
Prepared chicken broth	4 cups	1 L
Kernel corn	2 1/2 cups	625 mL
Chopped peeled potato	2 cups	500 mL
Diced red pepper	1 cup	250 mL
Sliced green onion	1/2 cup	125 mL
Sprigs of fresh thyme	2	2
Bay leaf	1	1
Salt	1/4 tsp.	1 mL
Half-and-half cream	1 1/2 cups	375 mL
All-purpose flour	3 tbsp.	45 mL
Chopped green onion, for garnish		

Heat cooking oil in a Dutch oven or large pot on medium. Add next 5 ingredients and cook, uncovered, for about 10 minutes, stirring occasionally, until turkey is no longer pink and vegetables are softened.

Stir in next 8 ingredients and bring to a boil. Reduce heat to medium-low. Simmer, covered, for about 15 minutes until potato is tender.

Whisk cream and flour in a small bowl until smooth. Stir into soup. Increase heat to medium. Cook, stirring, for about 5 minutes until boiling and thickened. Discard thyme sprigs and bay leaf. Garnish individual servings with green onion. Makes about 10 cups (2.5 L).

1 cup (250 mL): 300 Calories; 14 g Total Fat (2.5 g Mono, 1.5 g Poly, 6 g Sat); 60 mg Cholesterol; 22 g Carbohydrate (2 g Fibre, 3 g Sugar); 21 g Protein; 680 mg Sodium

Hot and Sour Turkey Pot Soup

This slow-cooker turkey soup is so comforting, and it has just the right blend of spicy and sour ingredients to perk you up in no time.

Chinese dried mushrooms	6	6
Boiling water	1 cup	250 mL
Prepared chicken broth	4 cups	1 L
Diced cooked turkey (see Tip, page 62)	2 cups	500 mL
Sliced carrot	2 cups	500 mL
Cubed firm tofu	1 cup	250 mL
Sliced celery	1 cup	250 mL
Soy sauce	1/4 cup	60 mL
Rice vinegar	2 tbsp.	30 mL
Chili paste (sambal oelek)	1 tsp.	5 mL
Prepared chicken broth	1/4 cup	60 mL
Cornstarch	2 tbsp.	30 mL
Sesame oil (optional)	1 tsp.	5 mL
Chopped baby bok choy	2 cups	500 mL
Thinly sliced green onion	1/4 cup	60 mL
Rice vinegar	1 tbsp.	15 mL

Put mushrooms into a small heatproof bowl and add boiling water. Stir gently and let stand for about 20 minutes until softened. Drain. Remove and discard stems. Slice mushrooms into thin strips. Transfer to 3 1/2 to 4 quart (3.5 to 4 L) slow cooker.

Add next 8 ingredients. Stir well. Cook, covered, on Low for 4 to 6 hours or High for 2 to 3 hours until carrot is tender.

Combine next 3 ingredients in a small bowl. Add to slow cooker and stir gently.

Add bok choy and green onion. Stir well. Cook, covered, on High for about 5 minutes until slightly thickened.

Stir in second amount of vinegar. Makes about 8 cups (2 L).

1 cup (250 mL): 160 Calories; 6 g Total Fat (1.5 g Mono, 2.5 g Poly, 1 g Sat); 20 mg Cholesterol; 12 g Carbohydrate (2 g Fibre, 4 g Sugar); 14 g Protein; 1140 mg Sodium

Artichoke Shrimp Soup

Round out this creamy, easy-to-prepare soup with a salad and some fresh baguettes for dunking. A bottle of wine and a light dessert is all you need to finish off the menu.

Butter (or hard margarine)	1 tbsp.	15 mL
Finely chopped onion	1/4 cup	60 mL
Finely chopped celery	1/2 cup	125 mL
Can of artichoke hearts (14 oz., 398 mL), drained and chopped	1	1
Garlic cloves, minced (or 1/2 tsp., 2 mL powder)	2	2
Low-sodium prepared chicken broth	1 1/2 cups	375 mL
Frozen, cooked shrimp (peeled and deveined), thawed and chopped	4 1/2 oz.	127 g
Half-and-half cream	1 1/4 cup	300 mL
Chopped fresh basil	1 tbsp.	15 mL

Melt butter in a large saucepan on medium. Add onion and celery. Cook, uncovered, for about 5 minutes, stirring often, until onion is softened.

Add artichoke hearts and garlic. Cook, stirring, for 1 to 2 minutes until garlic is fragrant.

Stir in broth. Cook, uncovered, for about 10 minutes, stirring occasionally, until heated through.

Add shrimp and cream. Cook, stirring, for about 1 minute until heated through. Transfer to a serving bowl.

Sprinkle with basil. Makes about 4 1/2 cups (1.1 L).

1 cup (250 mL): 200 Calories; 12 g Total Fat (4 g Mono, 1.5 g Poly, 6 g Sat); 90 mg Cholesterol; 11 g Carbohydrate (4 g Fibre, 2 g Sugar); 12 g Protein; 710 mg Sodium

Tom Yum Soup

This hot and spicy Thai specialty features ginger, lemon grass and lime. Use fewer red chilies if you like a milder soup.

Prepared chicken broth	4 cups	1 L
Thinly sliced fresh shiitake mushrooms	1 cup	250 mL
Ginger root slices (1/4 inch, 6 mm, thick)	3	3
Lemon grass, bulbs only (roots and stalks removed)	3	3
Uncooked medium shrimp (peeled and deveined)	3/4 lb.	340 g
Can of shoestring-style bamboo shoots (8 oz., 227 mL), drained	1	1
Thai hot chili peppers, chopped (see Tip, below)	3	3
Lime juice	3 tbsp.	45 mL
Fish sauce	2 tbsp.	30 mL
Chopped fresh cilantro (or parsley)	2 tsp.	10 mL

Measure broth into a large saucepan and bring to a boil. Reduce heat to medium. Add mushrooms and ginger root. Simmer, uncovered, for about 5 minutes until mushrooms are tender.

Pound lemon grass bulbs with a mallet or rolling pin until partially crushed. Add to broth mixture. Stir in next 3 ingredients. Simmer, uncovered, for about 2 minutes until shrimp turn pink. Remove from heat. Remove and discard ginger root and lemon grass.

Stir in remaining 3 ingredients. Makes about 5 cups (1.25 L).

1 cup (250 mL): 120 Calories; 1.5 g Total Fat (0 g Mono, .5 g Poly, 0 g Sat); 105 mg Cholesterol; 10 g Carbohydrate (1 g Fibre, 4 g Sugar); 15 g Protein; 1030 mg Sodium

Tip: Hot peppers contain capsaicin in the seeds and ribs. Removing the seeds will reduce the heat. Wear rubber gloves when handling hot peppers and avoid touching your eyes. Wash your hands well afterwards.

Cioppino

An Italian fish stew, cioppino was traditionally made with whatever was left after the fisherman sold his catch. This version is richly flavoured with wine, lobster, shrimp, scallops and crab.

Medium leeks (white and tender parts only), thinly sliced	2	2
Garlic cloves, minced	3	3
Olive (or cooking) oil	2 tbsp.	30 mL
Butter (or hard margarine)	1 tbsp.	15 mL
Small fresh mushrooms, chopped	3 cups	750 mL)
Can of stewed tomatoes (14 oz., 398 mL), with juice, mashed	1	1
Dry (or alcohol-free) red wine	1 1/2 cups	375 mL
Can of tomato paste (5 1/2 oz., 156 mL)	1	1
Lemon juice	3 tbsp.	45 mL
Dried sweet basil	2 tsp.	10 mL
Dried thyme	1/2 tsp.	2 mL
Bay leaf	1	1
Uncooked lobster tail (about 8 oz., 225 g), cut into 1 inch (2.5 cm) pieces	1	1
Uncooked medium shrimp (about 8 oz., 225 g), peeled and deveined	24	24
Fresh (or frozen) small bay scallops (about 10 oz., 285 g)	1 1/2 cups	375 mL
King (or snow) crab legs, shelled, broken into pieces (or 9 oz., 255 g, imitation crab chunks)	1 lb.	454 g
No-salt seasoning	1/2 tsp.	2 mL
Pepper, to taste		

Sauté leek and garlic in olive oil and butter in a large frying pan until leek is soft.

Stir in next 8 ingredients and bring to a boil. Transfer to a 4 to 5 quart (4 to 5 L) slow cooker. Cook, covered, on Low for 6 to 7 hours, or on High for 3 to 3 1/2 hours. Remove and discard bay leaf.

Stir in remaining 6 ingredients. Cook, covered, on High for 20 to 30 minutes. Makes 6 servings.

1 serving: 340 Calories; 9 g Total Fat (4 g Mono, 1.5 g Poly, 2 g Sat); 125 mg Cholesterol; 25 g Carbohydrate (4 g Fibre, 9 g Sugar); 32 g Protein; 820 mg Sodium

Wonton Soup

The shrimp-filled dumplings in this delicious ginger and onion broth are a unique variation of the everyday wonton soup. For a more traditional wonton soup, substitute 1/2 lb. (225 g) ground pork for the shrimp.

Frozen uncooked shrimp (peeled and deveined), thawed	1/2 lb.	225 g
Chopped green onion	1/4 cup	60 mL
Soy sauce	2 tsp.	10 mL
Cornstarch	2 tsp.	10 mL
Garlic clove, minced (or 1/4 tsp., 1 mL, powder)	1	1
Finely grated ginger root	1 tsp.	5 mL
Sesame oil (optional)	1 tsp.	5 mL
Water	1/4 cup	60 mL
Cornstarch	1 tbsp.	15 mL
Round dumpling wrappers, thawed	48	48
Prepared chicken broth	6 cups	1.5 L
Water	1 cup	250 mL
Dry sherry	1 tbsp.	15 mL
Sesame oil (optional)	1 tsp.	5 mL
Piece of ginger root (1/2 inch, 12 mm, length)	1	1
Sliced fresh mushrooms	1/2 cup	125 mL
Chopped green onion	1/4 cup	60 mL
Sliced suey choy (optional)	1 cup	250 mL

Put first 7 ingredients into a food processor. Process with on/off motion until shrimp is finely chopped. Set aside.

Stir water into second amount of cornstarch in a small bowl until smooth.

Place 8 wrappers on a work surface. Cover remaining wrappers with a damp towel to prevent them from drying out. Place about 1 tsp. (5 mL) shrimp mixture slightly off-centre on one side of each wrapper. Dampen edges of wrappers with cornstarch mixture. Fold in half over filling and crimp edges to seal. Cover filled wontons with a damp towel to prevent them from drying out. Repeat, in batches, with remaining wrappers and filling.

Put next 5 ingredients into a large saucepan and bring to a boil. Add wontons and return to a boil. Reduce heat to medium. Boil gently, uncovered, for 5 minutes.

Add mushrooms, green onion and suey choy, if using. Cook for about 3 minutes until wontons are tender and filling is pink. Remove and discard ginger root. Makes about 9 cups (2.25 L).

1 cup (250 mL): 120 Calories; 3 g Total Fat (.5 g Mono, 1 g Poly, .5 g Sat); 50 mg Cholesterol; 13 g Carbohydrate (0 g Fibre, 1 g Sugar); 9 g Protein; 1230 mg Sodium

Cajun Jumbo

Loaded with shrimp, chicken, sausage, rice and okra, this delicious jumbo is a meal in itself. Use a spicy sausage and increase the cayenne and hot pepper sauce if you like your food spicy.

All-purpose flour	1/3 cup	75 mL
Paprika	2 tsp.	10 mL
Dried thyme	1 tsp.	5 mL
Boneless, skinless chicken breast halves, cut into 3/4 inch (2 cm) cubes	1/2 lb.	225 g
Cooking oil	1/3 cup	75 mL
Diced onion	1 1/2 cups	375 mL
Diced green pepper	1 1/2 cups	375 mL
Diced celery	1 cup	250 mL
Prepared chicken broth	4 cups	1 L
Dry (or alcohol-free) white wine	1/2 cup	125 mL
Can of diced tomatoes (14 oz., 398 mL), with juice	1	1
Package of frozen okra (8 1/2 oz., 250 g), thawed and cut into 1/2 inch (12 mm) pieces	1	1
Smoked sausage, chopped	6 oz.	170 g
Long grain white rice	1/2 cup	125 mL
Bay leaf	1	1
Dried oregano	1 tsp.	5 mL
Salt	1/2 tsp.	2 mL
Pepper	1/4 tsp.	1 mL
Cayenne pepper	1/4 tsp.	1 mL
Frozen uncooked medium shrimp (peeled and deveined), thawed	1/2 lb.	225 g
Hot pepper sauce	1/2 tsp.	2 mL

Combine first 3 ingredients in a large resealable plastic bag. Add chicken, seal bag and toss until chicken is well coated. Transfer chicken to a large plate. Reserve remaining flour mixture.

Heat cooking oil in a Dutch oven or large pot on medium. Add chicken and cook for about 5 minutes, stirring occasionally, until starting to brown.

Stir in next 3 ingredients. Cook for about 5 to 10 minutes, stirring often, until vegetables start to soften. Sprinkle with reserved flour mixture. Cook, stirring, for 1 minute.

Slowly add broth and wine, stirring constantly and scraping any brown bits from bottom of pan until boiling and thickened.

Stir in next 9 ingredients and bring to a boil. Reduce heat to medium-low. Simmer, partially covered, for about 35 minutes, stirring occasionally, until vegetables are very tender. Remove and discard bay leaf.

Stir in shrimp and hot pepper sauce. Cook, covered, for 2 to 3 minutes until shrimp turn pink. Makes about 6 servings.

1 serving: *400 Calories; 16 g Total Fat (4.5 g Mono, 8 g Poly, 1 g Sat); 80 mg Cholesterol; 34 g Carbohydrate (4 g Fibre, 6 g Sugar); 26 g Protein; 1120 mg Sodium*

Spicy Coconut Rice Soup

If you are a fan of coconut rice, then this coconut soup is for you. Chock full of vegetables and shrimp, it comes with a spicy kick.

Canola oil	1 tsp.	5 mL
Chopped onion	1 cup	250 mL
Red curry paste	1 tsp.	5 mL
Prepared chicken broth	5 cups	1.25 L
Granulated sugar	1 tbsp.	15 mL
Soy sauce	1 tbsp.	15 mL
Wild rice	1/4 cup	60 mL
Long grain brown rice	1/4 cup	60 mL
Can of cut baby corn (14 oz., 398 mL), drained	1	1
Sliced red pepper	1 cup	250 mL
Snow peas, trimmed and halved	1 cup	250 mL
Can of light coconut milk (14 oz., 398 mL)	1	1
Frozen, uncooked medium shrimp (peeled and deveined), thawed	1/2 lb.	225 g
Lime juice	1 tbsp.	15 mL

Heat canola oil in a large saucepan on medium. Add onion and cook, uncovered, for about 5 minutes, stirring often, until onion starts to soften.

Add curry paste and cook, stirring, for about 1 minute until fragrant.

Stir in next 3 ingredients and bring to a boil.

Add wild rice. Reduce heat to medium-low and simmer, covered, for 30 minutes. Bring to a boil.

Stir in brown rice and reduce heat to medium-low. Simmer, covered, for about 30 minutes until rice is tender.

Stir in next 3 ingredients. Simmer, covered, for about 3 minutes until vegetables are tender-crisp.

Stir in coconut milk and shrimp. Simmer, covered, for about 2 minutes until shrimp turn pink. Stir in lime juice. Makes about 8 cups (2 L).

1 cup (250 mL): *160 Calories; 4.5 g Total Fat (0 g Mono, 0 g Poly, 2.5 g Sat); 40 mg Cholesterol; 20 g Carbohydrate (2 g Fibre, 5 g Sugar); 9 g Protein; 670 mg Sodium*

Manhattan Clam Chowder

This tomato-based chowder is a variation of the richer, cream-based New England version.

Bacon slices, diced	3	3
Finely chopped onion	1 cup	250 mL
Finely diced celery	1 cup	250 mL
Water	3 cups	750 mL
Diced potato	2 cups	500 mL
Can of diced tomatoes (14 oz., 398 mL), with juice	1	1
Diced carrot	1 cup	250 mL
Reserved clam liquid	1/2 cup	125 mL
Parsley flakes	2 tsp.	10 mL
Salt	3/4 tsp.	4 mL
Pepper	1/8 tsp.	0.5 mL
Ground marjoram	1/2 tsp.	2 mL
Ground thyme	1/4 tsp.	1 mL
Water	2 tbsp.	30 mL
Cornstarch	2 tbsp.	30 mL
Cans of whole baby clams (5 oz., 142 g, each), drained and liquid reserved	2	2

Cook bacon in a large saucepan on medium until almost crisp. Drain all but 2 tsp. (10 mL) drippings. Add onion and celery. Cook for 5 to 10 minutes, stirring often, until onion is softened.

Stir in next 10 ingredients. Cook, covered, for 10 to 15 minutes until potato and carrot are tender.

Stir water into cornstarch in a small cup until smooth. Slowly add to soup, stirring constantly, until boiling and thickened.

Stir in clams. Cook, uncovered, for about 10 minutes, stirring occasionally, until heated through. Makes about 8 cups (2 L).

1 cup (250 mL): 100 Calories; 2 g Total Fat (0.5 g Mono, 0.5 g Poly, 0.5 g Sat); 15 mg Cholesterol; 16 g Carbohydrate (2 g Fibre, 4 g Sugar); 6 g Protein; 560 mg Sodium

Boston Clam Chowder

A Company's Coming classic! Dill adds a fresh accent to the clam and smoky bacon flavours.

Bacon slices, diced	4	4
Chopped onion	1 cup	250 mL
Diced celery	1/2 cup	125 mL
All-purpose flour	1/4 cup	60 mL
Cans of whole baby clams (5 oz., 142 g each)	2	2
Water	1 cup	250 mL
Diced peeled potato	3 cups	750 mL
Bay leaf	1	1
Salt	1/2 tsp.	2 mL
Pepper	1/4 tsp.	1 mL
Ground thyme	1/4 tsp.	1 mL
Milk	2 cups	500 mL
Chopped fresh dill (or 1 1/2 tsp., 7 mL, dill weed)	2 tbsp.	30 mL

Cook bacon in a large saucepan on medium until almost crisp. Add onion and celery. Cook for about 5 minutes, stirring occasionally, until onion is softened.

Sprinkle with flour. Cook, stirring, for 1 minute.

Drain clams, reserving 1 cup (250 mL) liquid. Cover clams and set aside in refrigerator. Add clam liquid and water to saucepan. Cook, stirring, until boiling and thickened.

Stir in next 5 ingredients and bring to a boil. Reduce heat to medium-low. Simmer, covered, for about 20 minutes, stirring occasionally, until potato is tender.

Add clams, milk and dill. Cook for about 5 minutes, stirring often, until heated through. Remove and discard bay leaf. Makes about 8 cups (2 L).

1 cup (250 mL): 140 Calories; 3 g Total Fat (1 g Mono, 0 g Poly, 1 g Sat); 20 mg Cholesterol; 20 g Carbohydrate (1 g Fibre, 5 g Sugar); 9 g Protein; 310 mg Sodium

Crab Asparagus Soup

An egg drop-style soup with sophisticated flavours, this dish whips up quickly with easy-to-find ingredients.

Cooking oil	1 tsp.	5 mL
Sliced fresh white mushrooms	1/2 cup	125 mL
Chopped green onion	1/4 cup	60 mL
Garlic clove, minced	1	1
(or 1/4 tsp., 1 mL, powder)		
Finely grated, peeled ginger root	1/4 tsp.	1 mL
Pepper	1/4 tsp.	1 mL
Prepared chicken broth	3 cups	750 mL
Fresh asparagus, trimmed of tough ends,	1/2 lb.	225 g
cut into 1 inch (2.5 cm) pieces		
Can of crabmeat (6 oz., 170 g), drained,	1	1
cartilage removed, flaked		
Cornstarch	2 tsp.	10 mL
Soy sauce	2 tsp.	10 mL
Hoisin sauce	2 tsp.	10 mL
Large egg	1	1
Water	1 tbsp.	15 mL

Heat cooking oil in a medium saucepan on medium. Add next 5 ingredients and cook for 5 to 10 minutes, stirring often, until onion is softened.

Stir in broth and bring to a boil on medium-high.

Add asparagus and crabmeat. Reduce heat to medium and boil gently, covered, for about 5 minutes until asparagus is tender-crisp.

Combine next 3 ingredients in a small cup and add to soup. Cook, stirring, for about 1 minute until boiling and slightly thickened.

Beat egg and water with a fork in same small cup. Add to soup in a thin stream, stirring constantly. Makes about 4 1/2 cups (1.1 L).

1 cup (250 mL): 100 Calories; 3 g Total Fat (1 g Mono, .5 g Poly, .5 g Sat); 80 mg Cholesterol; 6 g Carbohydrate (1 g Fibre, 3 g Sugar); 13 g Protein; 760 mg Sodium

Mulligatawny Soup

Muhl-ih-guh-TAW-nee, which means "pepper water," is a traditional soup from India—a creamy, warmly spiced medley of potatoes, apples, lentils and onions. Garnish with yogurt and sprigs of fresh cilantro.

Chopped onion	1 1/2 cups	375 mL
Garlic cloves, minced	2	2
(or 1/2 tsp., 2 mL, powder)		
Finely grated ginger root	2 tsp.	10 mL
(or 1/2 tsp., 2 mL, ground ginger)		
Fresh small chilies, chopped	2	2
(see Tip, page 92)		
Curry powder	1/2 tbsp.	7 mL
Ground cumin	1 tsp.	5 mL
Ground coriander	1 tsp.	5 mL
Canola oil	2 tsp.	10 mL
Cinnamon stick (4 inch, 10 cm, length)	1	1
Whole green cardamom, bruised	7	7
(see Tip, below)		
Red lentils	1 1/4 cups	300 mL
Prepared vegetable broth	8 cups	2 L
Medium potatoes, peeled and chopped	2	2
Medium cooking apples (such as McIntosh),	2	2
peeled, cored and chopped		
Buttermilk	1 1/2 cups	375 mL
Fresh cilantro leaves	3 tbsp.	45 mL

Sauté first 7 ingredients in canola oil in large pot or Dutch oven for about 5 minutes until onion is soft.

Stir in next 6 ingredients. Bring to a boil. Reduce heat to medium-low. Simmer, covered, for about 25 minutes, stirring occasionally, until lentils and potato are soft. Cool slightly. Remove and discard cinnamon stick and cardamom. Following manufacturer's instructions for processing hot liquids, carefully process with a hand blender, or in a blender in batches, until smooth. Return to pot.

Add buttermilk and cilantro. Heat, stirring, on medium for 5 to 7 minutes until heated through. Makes about 12 cups (3 L).

1 cup (250 mL): 160 Calories; 1.5 g Total Fat (0 g Mono, 0.5 g Poly, 0 g Sat); 0 mg Cholesterol; 28 g Carbohydrate (5 g Fibre, 6 g Sugar); 7 g Protein; 660 mg Sodium

Tip: To bruise cardamom, pound pods with mallet or press with flat side of wide knife to "bruise," or crack them open slightly.

Miso Soup with Noodles

Miso is the basis for many tasty Japanese dishes. It comes in several varieties—the lighter the colour, the more delicate the flavour. Although you can use any variety of miso, we went all out and used red miso because the stronger flavour combines well with the hot chili. For those who like a saltier flavour, serve soy sauce on the side.

Water	1/4 cup	60 mL
Dry sherry	2 tbsp.	30 mL
Miso	2 tbsp.	30 mL
Granulated sugar	1 tsp.	5 mL
Chili paste (sambal oelek)	1/2 tsp.	2 mL
Sesame oil	2 tsp.	10 mL
Grated carrot	3 tbsp.	45 mL
Green onions, sliced	2	2
Finely grated ginger root	1 tsp.	5 mL
Small garlic clove, minced	1	1
Water	2 1/2 cups	625 mL
Prepared vegetable broth	1 1/2 cups	375 mL
Shredded fresh spinach leaves, lightly packed	1/2 cup	125 mL
Firm tofu, cut into 1/2 inch (12 mm) pieces	3 oz.	85 g
Rice vermicelli, broken up, softened according to package directions	1 1/2 oz.	43 g

Whisk first 5 ingredients in a small bowl. Set aside.

Heat sesame oil in a large saucepan on medium. Add next 4 ingredients and cook, stirring, for about 2 minutes until fragrant.

Add second amount of water and broth. Bring to a boil. Add miso mixture. Reduce heat to medium and boil gently, uncovered, for 2 minutes.

Stir in remaining 3 ingredients. Remove from heat and let stand for about 3 minutes until spinach is wilted and tofu is heated through. Makes about 5 cups (1.25 L).

1 cup (250 mL): 100 Calories; 3.5 g Total Fat (1 g Mono, 1 g Poly, .5 g Sat); 0 mg Cholesterol; 12 g Carbohydrate (0 g Fibre, 2 g Sugar); 4 g Protein; 560 mg Sodium

Carrot Satay Soup

Don't tie yourself to the stove—this Thai delight is made in your slow cooker. Creamy carrots, peanut undertones and a gentle spicy heat make this soup vibrant and velvety.

Prepared vegetable broth	3 cups	750 mL
Sliced carrot	3 cups	750 mL
Chopped onion	1 cup	250 mL
Chopped celery	1/2 cup	125 mL
Brown sugar, packed	2 tbsp.	30 mL
Garlic cloves, minced (or 1/2 tsp., 2 mL, powder)	2	2
Finely grated ginger root	2 tsp.	10 mL
Salt	1/2 tsp.	2 mL
Cayenne pepper	1/8 tsp.	0.5 mL
Cream cheese, softened	1/4 cup	60 mL
Smooth peanut butter	3 tbsp.	45 mL
Soy sauce	1 tbsp.	15 mL
Sesame seeds, toasted (see Tip, below), for garnish		

Combine first 9 ingredients in a 3 1/2 to 4 quart (3.5 to 4 L) slow cooker. Cook, covered, on Low for 5 to 6 hours or on High for 2 1/2 to 3 hours until vegetables are tender.

Add next 3 ingredients. Following manufacturer's instructions for processing hot liquids, carefully process with a hand blender, or in a blender in batches, until smooth.

Garnish individual servings with sesame seeds. Makes about 6 cups (1.5 L).

1 cup (250 mL): 130 Calories; 4.5 g Total Fat (0 g Mono, 0 g Poly, 1 g Sat); 0 mg Cholesterol; 18 g Carbohydrate (3 g Fibre, 11 g Sugar); 4 g Protein; 980 mg Sodium

Tip: To toast nuts, seeds or coconut, place them in an ungreased shallow frying pan. Heat on medium for 3 to 5 minutes, stirring often, until golden. To bake, spread them evenly in an ungreased shallow pan. Bake in a 350°F (175°C) oven for 5 to 10 minutes, stirring or shaking often, until golden.

Tomato and Zucchini Soup

ok best not great.

Caramelized onion adds a simple sweetness to this satisfying tomato soup. Once the onions have been caramelized, the rest of the soup comes together quickly. Take care not to overcook the zucchini. You want it to be tender, not mushy.

Ingredient	Imperial	Metric
Olive (or cooking) oil	1 tbsp.	15 mL
Thinly sliced onion	2 cups	500 mL
Red wine vinegar	2 tsp.	10 mL
Granulated sugar	2 tsp.	10 mL
Pepper	1/4 tsp.	1 mL
Can of diced tomatoes (28 oz., 796 mL), with juice	1	1
Low-sodium prepared vegetable broth	2 cups	500 mL
Medium zucchini (with peel), chopped	2	2
Kernel corn	1 cup	250 mL
Chopped fresh basil	1/4 cup	60 mL

Heat olive oil in a large saucepan on medium. Add onion and cook for about 20 minutes, stirring often, until caramelized.

Add next 3 ingredients. Cook, stirring, for about 1 minute until sugar is dissolved.

Stir in next 4 ingredients and bring to a boil on medium-high. Reduce heat to medium-low. Simmer, covered, for 5 to 10 minutes, stirring occasionally, until zucchini is tender.

Stir in basil. Makes 6 servings.

1 serving: 100 Calories; 2.5 g Total Fat (1.5 g Mono, 0 g Poly, 0 g Sat); 0 mg Cholesterol; 20 g Carbohydrate (2 g Fibre, 10 g Sugar); 3 g Protein; 610 mg Sodium

Easy Minestrone

Minestrone soup is another of those classic Italian soups that started out as a way for poor farmers to make a meal out of whatever veggies they had on hand. Traditionally, minestrone soups contained fresh vegetables and beans but no meat. Today many recipes include beef, but in this dish we present a delicious meat-free soup that is true to its roots.

Olive (or cooking) oil	1 tbsp.	15 mL
Chopped cabbage	1 cup	250 mL
Finely chopped celery	1/2 cup	125 mL
Finely chopped onion	1/2 cup	125 mL
Sliced carrot	1/2 cup	125 mL
Diced red pepper	1/3 cup	75 mL
Garlic clove, minced (or 1/4 tsp., 1 mL, powder)	1	1
Prepared vegetable broth	6 cups	1.5 L
Can of mixed beans (19 oz., 540 mL), rinsed and drained	1	1
Can of stewed tomatoes (14 oz., 398 mL), cut up	1	1
Tomato paste (see Tip, page 18)	2 tbsp.	30 mL
Parsley flakes	1 tbsp.	15 mL
Dried basil	1/2 tsp.	2 mL
Dried oregano	1/2 tsp.	2 mL
Ditali pasta (or elbow macaroni)	1/3 cup	75 mL
Salt	1/4 tsp.	1 mL
Grated Parmesan cheese (see Tip, below)	2 tbsp.	30 mL

Heat olive oil in a large saucepan on medium-high. Add next 6 ingredients. Cook for about 5 minutes, stirring often, until vegetables start to soften and brown.

Stir in next 7 ingredients and bring to a boil. Reduce heat to medium. Boil gently, partially covered, for about 15 minutes until vegetables are tender.

Stir in pasta and salt. Boil gently, uncovered, for about 12 minutes, stirring occasionally, until pasta is tender.

Sprinkle individual servings with cheese. Makes about 9 cups (2.25 L).

1 cup (250 mL): 130 Calories; 2.5 g Total Fat (1 g Mono, 0 g Poly, 2.5 g Sat); 0 mg Cholesterol; 23 g Carbohydrate (5 g Fibre, 6 g Sugar); 6 g Protein; 940 mg Sodium

Tip: Authentic Parmesan cheese is not vegetarian, so leave it out or choose a vegetarian Paremsan-type cheese if you are serving this dish to vegetarians.

Garden Fresh Tomato Soup

Forget the canned tomatoes—this soup is a tangy treat full of fresh veggies. It is the perfect dish for when your kitchen is overflowing with all your harvested garden tomatoes. If you prefer a cream of tomato soup, add 1/2 cup (125 mL) whipping cream to the soup after it has been blended and heat it on the stovetop until it is warmed through. Garnish with fresh parsley for an attractive presentation.

Cooking oil	2 tsp.	10 mL
Chopped onion	1 cup	250 mL
Chopped carrot	1/2 cup	125 mL
Chopped celery	1/2 cup	125 mL
Garlic cloves, minced (or 1/2 tsp., 2 mL, powder)	2	2
Medium tomatoes (about 3 lbs., 1.4 kg), peeled, seeded and chopped (see Tip, page 119)	8	8
Prepared vegetable broth	1 cup	250 mL
Tomato paste (see Tip, page 18)	2 tbsp.	30 mL
Granulated sugar	2 tsp.	10 mL
Dried basil	1/2 tsp.	2 mL
Dried oregano	1/2 tsp.	2 mL
Dried thyme	1/2 tsp.	2 mL
Bay leaf	1	1
Salt	1/2 tsp.	2 mL
Pepper	1/2 tsp.	2 mL

Heat cooking oil in a saucepan on medium. Add next 4 ingredients. Cook for 5 to 10 minutes, stirring occasionally, until vegetables are softened.

Stir in remaining 10 ingredients and bring to a boil. Reduce heat to medium-low. Simmer, covered, for about 30 minutes, stirring occasionally, until vegetables are very soft. Remove and discard bay leaf. Following manufacturer's instructions for processing hot liquids, carefully process with a hand blender, or in a blender in batches, until smooth. Makes about 5 cups (1.25 L).

1 cup (250 mL): 80 Calories; 2.5 g Total Fat (1 g Mono, 1 g Poly, 0 g Sat); 0 mg Cholesterol; 15 g Carbohydrate (4 g Fibre, 9 g Sugar); 3 g Protein; 470 mg Sodium

Tip: To peel tomatoes, cut an "X" on the bottom of each tomato, just through the skin. Place tomatoes in boiling water for 30 seconds. Immediately transfer to a bowl of ice water. Let stand until cool enough to handle. Peel and discard skins.

Spicy Roasted Red Pepper Soup

This smooth soup with red pepper sweetness and warming chipotle heat can be served hot or chilled. Creamy buttermilk provides the perfect contrast for the smoky, sweet flavours of roasted red pepper.

Cooking oil	1 tsp.	5 mL
Sliced leek (white part only)	1 cup	250 mL
Chopped celery	1/2 cup	125 mL
Dried basil	1/2 tsp.	2 mL
Garlic clove, minced	1	1
Salt	1/4 tsp.	1 mL
Pepper	1/4 tsp.	1 mL
Prepared vegetable broth	3 cup	750 mL
Chopped roasted red pepper	1 1/2 cups	375 mL
Granulated sugar	1 1/2 tsp.	7 mL
Finely chopped chipotle peppers in adobo sauce (see Tip, below)	1/2 tsp.	2 mL
Cooked quinoa	1 cup	250 mL
Buttermilk	1/2 cup	125 mL

Heat cooking oil in a large saucepan on medium. Add leek and celery and cook for about 8 minutes, stirring often, until leek is golden and celery starts to soften.

Add next 4 ingredients and cook, stirring, for about 1 minute until garlic is fragrant.

Stir in next 5 ingredients and bring to a boil. Reduce heat to medium-low and simmer, covered, for about 20 minutes until celery is soft. Following manufacturer's instructions for processing hot liquids, carefully process with a hand blender, or in a blender in batches, until smooth.

Stir in buttermilk. Makes about 5 cups (1.25 L)

1 cup (250 mL): 110 Calories; 2.5 g Total Fat (.5 g Mono, 0 g Poly, 0 g Sat); 0 mg Cholesterol; 18 g Carbohydrate (2 g Fibre, 6 g Sugar); 3 g Protein; 910 mg Sodium

Tip: Chipotle peppers are smoked jalapeño peppers. Be sure to wash your hands after handling them. Store leftover chipotle peppers with their sauce in an airtight container in the refrigerator for up to 1 year.

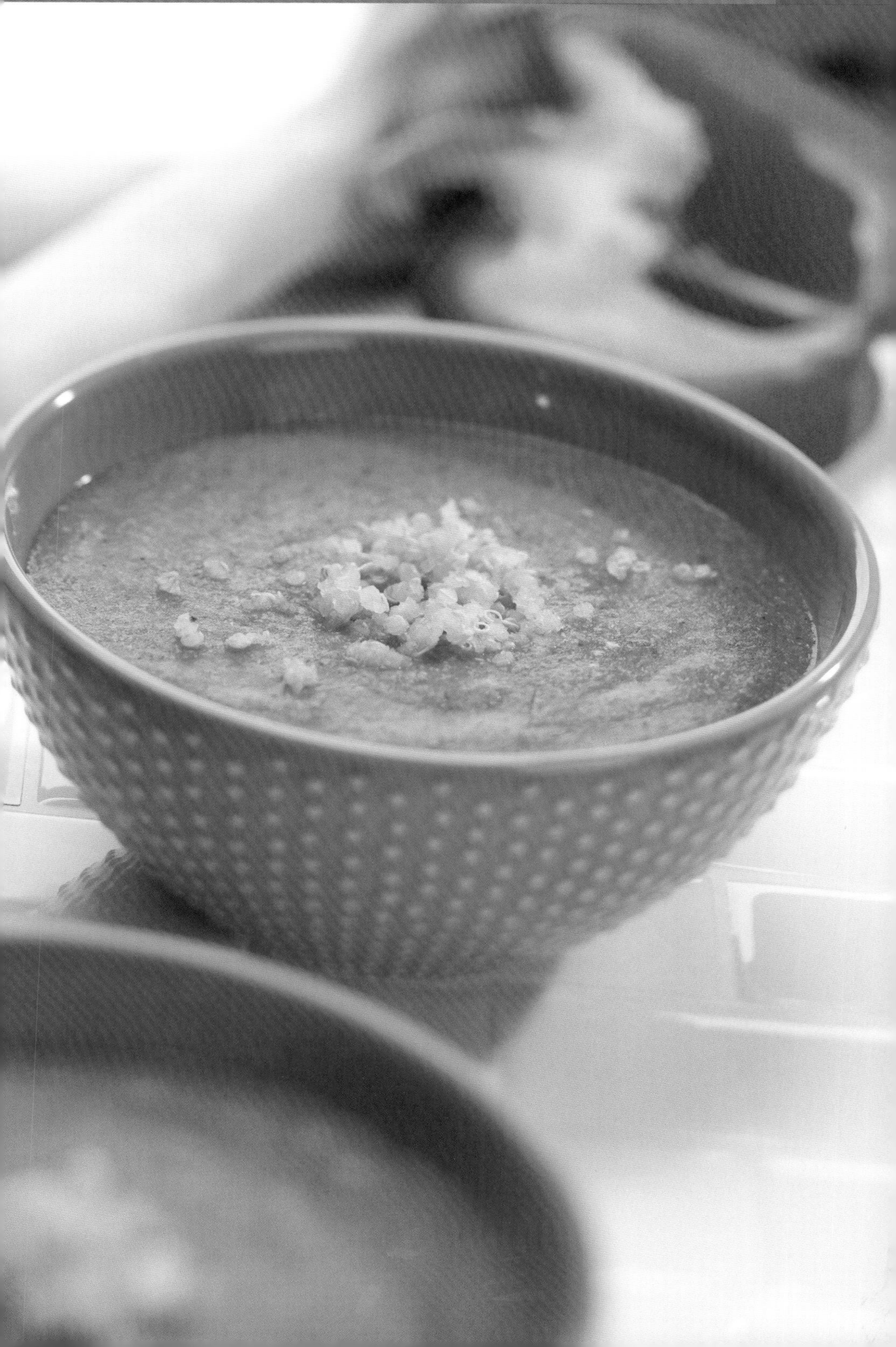

Borscht

With its classic combination of earthy beets, potatoes and cabbage, this soup is soothing in the cold winter months. For a traditional presentation, dish it up in white bowls to set off the lovely colour and top each with a dollop of sour cream and a sprinkle of fresh dill.

Cooking oil	1 tbsp.	15 mL
Chopped onion	1 cup	250 mL
Prepared vegetable broth	8 cups	2 L
Diced fresh peeled beets (see Tip, below)	3 cups	750 mL
Chopped carrot	1/4 cup	60 mL
Chopped celery	1/4 cup	60 mL
Dried dillweed	1/2 tsp.	2 mL
Salt	1 tsp.	5 mL
Pepper	1/4 tsp.	1 mL
Bay leaf	1	1
Diced peeled potato	1 cup	250 mL
Shredded green cabbage, lightly packed	1 cup	250 mL
Can of tomato paste (5 1/2 oz., 156 mL)	1	1
Lemon juice	2 tsp.	10 mL

Heat cooking oil in a Dutch oven on medium. Add onion and cook for about 5 minutes, stirring often, until softened.

Stir in next 8 ingredients and bring to a boil. Reduce heat to medium-low. Simmer, partially covered, for 20 minutes.

Add next 3 ingredients. Stir well. Simmer, partially covered, for about 25 minutes until vegetables are tender. Remove and discard bay leaf.

Stir in lemon juice. Makes about 9 1/2 cups (2.4 L).

1 cup (250 mL): 80 Calories; 1.5 g Total Fat (1 g Mono, 0 g Poly, 0 g Sat); 0 mg Cholesterol; 15 g Carbohydrate (3 g Fibre, 8 g Sugar); 2 g Protein; 1120 mg Sodium

Tip: Don't get caught red-handed! Wear rubber gloves when you are handling beets.

Cheddar Broccoli Soup

Satisfying and very easy to prepare, this remake of the traditional favourite gets its creaminess from potatoes.

Canola oil	2 tsp.	10 mL
Chopped broccoli	4 cups	1 L
Chopped unpeeled potato	4 cups	1 L
Chopped onion	1 cup	250 mL
Garlic cloves, minced (or 1/2 tsp., 2 mL, powder)	2	2
Prepared vegetable broth	6 cups	1.5 L
Grated sharp Cheddar cheese	2/3 cup	150 mL
Grated Parmesan cheese (see Tip, page 116)	1/4 cup	60 mL
Dijon mustard	2 tsp.	10 mL
Pepper	1/4 tsp.	1 mL

Heat canola oil in a Dutch oven on medium. Add next 4 ingredients and cook for about 10 minutes, stirring occasionally, until potato starts to soften.

Add broth and bring to a boil. Reduce heat to medium-low. Simmer, covered, for about 20 minutes until potato is tender. Remove from heat. Following manufacturer's instructions for processing hot liquids, carefully process with a hand blender, or in a blender in batches, until smooth.

Add remaining 4 ingredients. Stir until cheese is melted. Makes about 9 1/2 cups (2.4 L).

1 cup (250 mL): 140 Calories; 6 g Total Fat (2.5 g Mono, 1 g Poly, 2.5 g Sat); 10 mg Cholesterol; 16 g Carbohydrate (1 g Fibre, 2 g Sugar); 5 g Protein; 710 mg Sodium

Curried Cauliflower Chowder

This soup has plenty of curry flavor but is not overpowering. Add chopped apricots or dark raisins for a touch of sweetness.

Chopped onion	1 cup	250 mL
Diced green pepper	1/2 cup	125 mL
Chopped cauliflower	3 cups	750 mL
Water	2 cups	500 mL
Prepared vegetable broth	2 cups	500 mL
Light sour cream	1 cup	250 mL
Milk	1/2 cup	125 mL
Mashed potato	1/2 cup	125 mL
Curry powder	2 tsp.	10 mL
Salt	1/4 tsp.	1 mL
Pepper	1/8 tsp.	0.5 mL

Cook onion, green pepper and cauliflower in water in a large saucepan or Dutch oven until tender. Do not drain.

Stir in remaining 7 ingredients. Reduce heat to medium-low and simmer, covered, for 2 to 3 minutes. Makes 5 cups (1.25 L).

1 cup (250 mL): 130 Calories; 6 g Total Fat (1.5 g Mono, 0 g Poly, 3.5 g Sat); 20 mg Cholesterol; 16 g Carbohydrate (2 g Fibre, 5 g Sugar); 0 g Protein; 630 mg Sodium

Roasted Tomato Soup

Tomato soup and grilled cheese sandwiches—together at last! Garnish with green onions or parsley for an extra splash of colour.

Medium tomatoes, halved and seeded	12	12
Medium onions, cut into 8 wedges each	2	2
Cooking oil	2 tbsp.	30 mL
Garlic cloves, halved	3	3
Dried thyme	1 tsp.	5 mL
Pepper	1/2 tsp.	2 mL
Can of diced tomatoes (28 oz., 796 mL), with juice	1	1
Prepared vegetable broth	3 cups	750 mL
Water	1 cup	250 mL
Granulated sugar	2 tsp.	10 mL
Dry white wine (optional)	1/4 cup	60 mL
Butter (or hard margarine), softened	3 tbsp.	45 mL
Whole-wheat bread slices	6	6
Grated jalapeño Monterey Jack cheese	3/4 cup	175 mL

Combine first 6 ingredients in a large bowl, tossing until tomato and onion are well coated. Arrange in a single layer on a greased baking sheet with sides. Cook in 400°F (200°C) oven for about 45 minutes until tomato starts to brown on edges. Transfer to a Dutch oven.

Stir in next 4 ingredients and bring to a boil. Reduce heat to medium. Boil gently, partially covered, for 20 minutes to blend flavours. Following manufacturer's instructions for processing hot liquids, carefully process with a hand blender, or in a blender in batches, until smooth. Stir in wine, if using.

For the croutons, spread butter on one side of each bread slice. Sprinkle 1/4 cup (60 mL) cheese on unbuttered side of 3 slices. Top with remaining bread slices, butter side up. Heat a large frying pan on medium. Add sandwiches and cook for 2 to 3 minutes per side until bread is golden and cheese is melted. Transfer to a cutting board and let stand for 5 minutes. Cut into 1/2 inch (12 mm) squares. Scatter over individual servings of soup. Makes 4 servings.

1 serving: 470 Calories; 24 g Total Fat (7 g Mono, 2.5 g Poly, 10 g Sat); 45 mg Cholesterol; 54 g Carbohydrate (10 g Fibre, 20 g Sugar); 15 g Protein; 1190 mg Sodium

Lemon Lentil Soup

A fragrant soup with a tangy, creamy broth. Pick up some pita bread or pappadums for a fast culinary visit to India.

Cooking oil	1 tbsp.	15 mL
Chopped carrot	1 1/2 cups	375 mL
Chopped onion	1 1/2 cups	375 mL
Curry powder	1 1/2 tbsp.	25 mL
Prepared vegetable broth	6 cups	1.5 L
Can of lentils (19 oz., 540 mL), rinsed and drained	1	1
Can of coconut milk (14 oz., 398 mL)	1	1
Bay leaves	2	2
Fresh spinach leaves, lightly packed	2 cups	500 mL
Lemon juice	2 tbsp.	30 mL
Salt	1/4 tsp.	1 mL

Heat cooking oil in a Dutch oven or large pot on medium-high. Add carrot and onion. Cook, uncovered, for 5 to 10 minutes, stirring often, until onion is softened.

Add curry powder. Cook, stirring, for 1 to 2 minutes until fragrant.

Stir in next 4 ingredients and bring to a boil. Reduce heat to medium. Boil gently, covered, for about 5 minutes, stirring occasionally, until carrot is tender. Remove and discard bay leaves.

Add remaining 3 ingredients. Cook, stirring, for about 2 minutes until spinach is wilted. Makes about 11 cups (2.75 L).

1 cup (250 mL): 150 Calories; 9 g Total Fat (1 g Mono, 0 g Poly, 7 g Sat); 0 mg Cholesterol; 14 g Carbohydrate (3 g Fibre, 3 g Sugar); 4 g Protein; 670 mg Sodium

Spinach Garlic Soup

Indulge in this velvety smooth soup on a cold winter's day. It makes a wonderful starter or side dish.

Butter (or hard margarine)	2 tsp.	10 mL
Cooking oil	2 tsp.	10 mL
Sliced leek (white part only)	1 1/2 cups	375 mL
Diced peeled potato	1 cup	250 mL
Garlic cloves, minced (or 3/4 tsp., 4 mL, powder)	3	3

Fresh spinach leaves, lightly packed
    (or box of frozen spinach, 10 oz.,
    300 g, thawed and squeezed dry)
	10 cups	2.5 L

Ground nutmeg	1/8 tsp.	0.5 mL
Salt	1/4 tsp.	1 mL
Pepper	1/8 tsp.	0.5 mL
Prepared vegetable broth	4 cups	1 L
Whipping cream	1/4 cup	60 mL

Heat butter and cooking oil in a large saucepan on medium. Add next 3 ingredients and cook for about 10 minutes, stirring occasionally, until leek is softened.

Add next 4 ingredients. Cook for 2 to 4 minutes, stirring occasionally, until spinach is wilted.

Stir in broth and bring to a boil. Reduce heat to medium-low. Simmer, covered, for about 10 minutes until potato is tender. Following manufacturer's instructions for processing hot liquids, carefully process with a hand blender, or in a blender in batches, until smooth. Stir in cream. Makes about 4 servings.

1 serving: 1100 Calories; 6 g Total Fat (2 g Mono, .5 g Poly, 2.5 g Sat); 15 mg Cholesterol; 11 g Carbohydrate (2 g Fibre, 2 g Sugar); 2 g Protein; 720 mg Sodium

Squash and Lentil soup

This smooth golden-coloured soup has spicy hits of curry and ginger. Serve with warm naan for dipping.

Cooking oil	2 tsp.	10 mL
Chopped onion	2 cups	500 mL
Garlic cloves, minced	2	2
(or 1/2 tsp., 2 mL, powder)		
Finely grated ginger root	1 tsp.	5 mL
(or 1/4 tsp., 1 mL, ground ginger)		
Curry powder	1 tbsp.	15 mL
Prepared vegetable broth	6 cups	1.5 L
Chopped butternut squash	5 cups	1.25 L
(about 1 1/2 lbs., 680 g),		
see Tip, below		
Dried red split lentils	1 1/2 cups	375 mL
Plain yogurt	1/3 cup	75 mL

Heat cooking oil in a large frying pan on medium. Add next 3 ingredients and cook for 5 to 10 minutes, stirring often, until onion is softened.

Add curry powder. Cook, stirring, for 1 to 2 minutes until fragrant. Transfer to a 4 to 5 quart (4 to 5 L) slow cooker.

Stir in next 3 ingredients. Cook, covered, on Low for 6 to 8 hours or on High for 3 to 4 hours until lentils and squash are tender. Following manufacturer's instructions for processing hot liquids, carefully process with a hand blender, or in a blender in batches, until smooth.

Stir in yogurt. Cook, covered, on High for about 15 minutes until heated through. Makes about 9 1/2 cups (2.4 L).

1 cup (250 mL): 180 Calories; 2 g Total Fat (.5 g Mono, 0 g Poly, 0 g Sat); 0 mg Cholesterol; 33 g Carbohydrate (6 g Fibre, 6 g Sugar); 10 g Protein; 610 mg Sodium

Tip: Some people have an allergic reaction to raw squash flesh, so wear rubber gloves when cutting or handling butternut or acorn squash.

Stilton Cauliflower Soup

Blue cheese lovers will be in raptures over this velvety purée. Make sure the blue cheese you use is vegetarian if you are serving this dish to vegetarians. Some companies still produce "traditional rennet" varieties, which are not suitable for vegetarians.

Small head of cauliflower (about 1 lb., 454 g), cut into small florets	1	1
Butter (or hard margarine)	2 tbsp.	30 mL
Chopped onion	1 1/2 cups	375 mL
Chopped celery	1 cup	250 mL
Bay leaf	1	1
Ground sage	1/4 tsp.	1 mL
Salt	1/4 tsp.	1 mL
Pepper	1/4 tsp.	1 mL
All-purpose flour	1/4 cup	60 mL
Prepared vegetable broth	4 cups	1 L
Milk	1 cup	250 mL
Crumbled Stilton (or other blue) cheese	1/4 cup	60 mL

Cook 1 cup (250 mL) of cauliflower florets in boiling salted water in a small saucepan for about 2 minutes until tender-crisp. Drain. Plunge into ice water in a medium bowl. Let stand for 10 minutes until cold. Drain and set aside.

Melt butter in a large saucepan on medium. Stir in next 6 ingredients and remaining cauliflower. Cook, covered, for about 10 minutes, stirring occasionally, until onion is softened.

Sprinkle with flour. Cook, stirring, for 1 minute. Slowly add 2 cups (500 mL) broth. Cook, stirring, until boiling and thickened. Stir in milk and remaining broth and bring to a boil. Reduce heat to medium-low. Simmer, partially covered, for about 15 minutes, stirring occasionally, until cauliflower is tender. Remove and discard bay leaf. Following manufacturer's instructions for processing hot liquids, carefully process with a hand blender, or in a blender in batches, until smooth.

Add cheese and cook, stirring, until heated through. Sprinkle reserved cauliflower florets over top. Makes about 7 cups (1.75 L).

1 cup (250 mL): 120 Calories; 5 g Total Fat (1.5 g Mono, 0 g Poly, 3 g Sat); 15 mg Cholesterol; 15 g Carbohydrate (2 g Fibre, 7 g Sugar); 5 g Protein; 780 mg Sodium

Roasted Garlic Potato Soup

Almonds and roasted garlic add flavour and texture to this unusual soup. Your family will be nutty about it. Factor in extra time to roast the garlic.

Garlic bulbs	3	3
Cooking oil	1 tbsp.	15 mL
Chopped onion	1 cup	250 mL
Diced peeled potato	2 cups	500 mL
Salt	1/4 tsp.	1 mL
Dry (or alcohol-free) white wine	1/3 cup	75 mL
Prepared vegetable broth	4 cups	1 L
Bay leaf	1	1
Dried thyme	1/4 tsp.	1 mL
Pepper	1/4 tsp.	1 mL
Slivered almonds, toasted (see Tip, page 112)	1/2 cup	125 mL
Milk	3/4 cup	175 mL
Chopped fresh parsley	1/4 cup	60 mL

Trim 1/4 inch (6 mm) from garlic bulbs to expose tops of cloves, leaving bulbs intact. Wrap loosely in greased foil. Bake in 375°F (190°C) oven for about 45 minutes until tender. Let stand until cool enough to handle. Squeeze garlic bulbs to remove cloves from peel. Discard peel. Set cloves aside.

Heat cooking oil in a large saucepan on medium. Add onion and cook for 5 to 10 minutes until softened.

Stir in potato, salt and wine. Cook, stirring, on medium-high for about 2 minutes until wine is almost evaporated.

Stir in next 4 ingredients and bring to a boil. Reduce heat to medium-low. Simmer, covered, for 10 minutes. Add roasted garlic. Simmer, covered, for 5 to 10 minutes until potato is tender. Transfer to a large bowl. Cool slightly. Remove and discard bay leaf. Carefully transfer 2 cups (500 mL) soup to a blender or food processor.

Add almonds to blender. Following manufacturer's instructions for processing hot liquids, carefully process until smooth. Return to same saucepan. Process remaining soup in blender or food processor until smooth. Return to saucepan.

Add milk and parsley. Cook, stirring, on medium for 2 to 3 minutes until heated through. Makes about 7 cups (1.75 L).

1 cup (250 mL): 160 Calories; 6 g Total Fat (3.5 g Mono, 1.5 g Poly, .5 g Sat); 0 mg Cholesterol; 22 g Carbohydrate (2 g Fibre, 4 g Sugar); 5 g Protein; 110 mg Sodium

Cream of Mushroom Soup

Our delightfully creamy mushroom soup is perked up with dill, paprika and wine. A timeless favourite.

Butter (or hard margarine)	2 tbsp.	30 mL
Thinly sliced fresh brown (or white) mushrooms (about 1 1/2 lbs., 680 g)	10 cups	2.5 L
Butter (or hard margarine)	1 tbsp.	15 mL
Finely chopped onion	2 1/2 cups	625 mL
Chopped fresh dill (or 1 tbsp., 15 mL, dill weed)	1/4 cup	60 mL
Paprika	2 tsp.	10 mL
Salt	1/2 tsp.	2 mL
Pepper	1/4 tsp.	1 mL
All-purpose flour	1/4 cup	60 mL
Prepared vegetable broth	3 cups	750 mL
Dry (or alcohol-free) white wine	1/2 cup	125 mL
Half-and-half cream	1 cup	250 mL
Chopped fresh parsley	3 tbsp.	45 mL
Sour cream	1/4 cup	60 mL
Lemon juice	1 1/2 tbsp.	25 mL

Melt first amount of butter in a large saucepan on medium-high. Add mushrooms and cook for about 10 minutes, stirring often, until mushrooms are browned and liquid is evaporated.

Add next 6 ingredients. Cook, stirring, on medium until second amount of butter is melted. Cook, covered, for 5 to 10 minutes, stirring occasionally, until onion is softened.

Sprinkle with flour. Cook, stirring, for 1 minute. Slowly add 2 cups (500 mL) broth. Cook, stirring, until boiling and thickened. Stir in wine and remaining broth and bring to a boil. Reduce heat to medium-low. Simmer, covered, for 15 minutes, stirring occasionally, to blend flavours.

Stir in cream and parsley.

Combine sour cream and lemon juice in a small cup. Drizzle onto individual servings. Makes about 7 cups (1.75 L).

1 cup (250 mL): 190 Calories; 11 g Total Fat (2 g Mono, .5 g Poly, 7 g Sat); 35 mg Cholesterol; 16 g Carbohydrate (2 g Fibre, 6 g Sugar); 6 g Protein; 650 mg Sodium

Golden Split Pea Soup

This vegetarian split-pea soup gets its golden colour from sweet potato, yellow zucchini, corn and yellow split peas.

Cooking oil	2 tsp.	10 mL
Chopped onion	1 cup	250 mL
Grated carrot	1 cup	250 mL
Prepared vegetable broth	6 cups	1.5 L
Chopped yellow zucchini (with peel), (see Tip, below)	1 1/2 cups	375 mL
Chopped, peeled sweet potato (or yam)	1 cup	250 mL
Kernel corn	1 cup	250 mL
Yellow split peas, rinsed and drained	3/4 cup	175 mL
Dill weed	1/2 tsp.	2 mL
Turmeric	1/4 tsp.	1 mL
Dried thyme	1/4 tsp.	1 mL
Bay leaf	1	1

Heat cooking oil in a large saucepan on medium. Add onion and carrot and cook for 5 to 10 minutes, stirring often, until onion is softened.

Stir in remaining 9 ingredients and bring to a boil. Reduce heat to medium-low. Simmer, covered, for about 1 hour, stirring occasionally, until sweet potato is tender and split peas are very soft. Remove and discard bay leaf. Makes about 8 cups (2 L).

1 cup (250 mL): 90 Calories; 1.5 g Total Fat (1 g Mono, 0 g Poly, 0 g Sat); 0 mg Cholesterol; 17 g Carbohydrate (3 g Fibre, 5 g Sugar); 3 g Protein; 770 mg Sodium

Tip: If yellow zucchini is not available, use peeled green zucchini instead.

Cucumber Avocado Soup

Smooth and refreshing, this chilled soup is a lovely mix of cucumber, citrus flavours and fresh basil. Add sliced cucumber and fresh mint leaves for the perfect garnish.

Ripe medium avocado	1	1
Chopped, peeled English cucumber	4 cups	1 L
Water	1 cup	250 mL
Plain yogurt	1 1/2 cups	375 mL
Extra virgin olive oil	3 tbsp.	45 mL
Lime juice	3 tbsp.	45 mL
Garlic clove, minced	1	1
Ground cumin	1/2 tsp.	2 mL
Salt	1 tsp.	5 mL
Pepper	1/4 tsp.	1 mL
Finely sliced green onion	2 tbsp.	30 mL
Finely shredded fresh basil	2 tbsp.	30 mL

Cut avocado in half and remove pit. Scoop pulp into a blender or food processor. Discard peel. Add cucumber and water. Process until smooth.

Add next 7 ingredients and process until smooth. Transfer to a large bowl.

Stir in green onion and basil. Chill, covered, for at least 2 hours until cold. Makes about 5 cups (1.25 L).

1 cup (250 mL): 210 Calories; 17 g Total Fat (11 g Mono, 1.5 g Poly, 3.5 g Sat); 10 mg Cholesterol; 12 g Carbohydrate (4 g Fibre, 6 g Sugar); 5 g Protein; 290 mg Sodium

Butternut Apple Soup

The tastes of autumn unite—apple and roasted squash combine in a delicate soup that is delicious served chilled or hot. Garnish with toasted pecans for a special touch.

Cooking oil	1 tbsp.	15 mL
Chopped, peeled butternut squash (see Tip, page 134)	4 cups	1 L
Cooking oil	1 tbsp.	15 mL
Chopped, peeled cooking apple (such as McIntosh)	3 cups	750 mL
Chopped onion	1/2 cup	125 mL
Prepared chicken broth	5 cups	1.25 mL
Ground cardamom	1/2 tsp.	2 mL
Chopped pecans, toasted (see Tip, page 112), for garnish		

Drizzle first amount of cooking oil over squash in a large bowl and stir until squash is coated. Arrange in a single layer on an ungreased baking sheet with sides. Bake in 450°F (230°C) oven for about 20 minutes, stirring occasionally, until edges start to brown.

Heat second amount of cooking oil in a large saucepan on medium-high. Add apple and onion and cook for 5 to 10 minutes, stirring often, until onion is softened.

Stir in next 2 ingredients and squash and bring to a boil. Reduce heat to medium. Simmer, covered, for about 15 minutes, stirring occasionally, until squash and apple are tender. Following manufacturer's instructions for processing hot liquids, carefully process with a hand blender, or in a blender in batches, until smooth. Transfer to a large bowl. Cool at room temperature before covering. Chill for at least 2 hours until cold.

Garnish individual servings with pecans. Makes about 7 cups (1.75 L).

1 cup (250 mL): 120 Calories; 4.5 g Total Fat (3 g Mono, 1.5 g Poly, 0 g Sat); 0 mg Cholesterol; 19 g Carbohydrate (3 g Fibre, 9 g Sugar); 3 g Protein; 480 mg Sodium

Summer Gazpacho

The refreshing flavour of this chilled delight is perfectly balanced by the crunchy crouton garnish.

Baguette bread slices, 1 inch (2.5 cm) thick	2	2
Large tomatoes, peeled (see Tip, page 119), seeded and chopped	4	4
Chopped, peeled and seeded English cucumber	1 cup	250 mL
Chopped red pepper	1 cup	250 mL
Chopped red onion	1/2 cup	125 mL
Olive oil	2 1/2 tbsp.	37 mL
Red wine vinegar	2 1/2 tbsp.	37 mL
Garlic clove, minced	1	1
Lime juice	1 tbsp.	15 mL
Hot pepper sauce	1/2 tsp.	2 mL
Salt	1/2 tsp.	2 mL
Baguette bread slices, 1/2 inch (12 mm) thick	8	8
Olive oil	1 1/2 tsp.	7 mL

Put first amount of bread slices in a small bowl. Pour water over top to cover. Soak for about 5 minutes until very soft. Drain. Squeeze water from bread.

Combine next 10 ingredients in a large bowl. Process 3/4 cup (175 mL) tomato mixture in a blender or food processor until finely chopped. Transfer to a small bowl and set aside in refrigerator to chill. Add wet bread to remaining tomato mixture. Process in blender or food processor until smooth. Chill, covered, for at least 2 hours until cold. Pour into 4 individual soup bowls.

Arrange second amount of bread slices on ungreased baking sheet. Brush with second amount of olive oil. Broil on top rack in oven for about 1 minute per side until golden. Place 2 slices on each soup. Spoon reserved tomato mixture over bread. Makes 4 servings.

1 serving: 190 Calories; 11 g Total Fat (7 g Mono, 1.5 g Poly, 1.5 g Sat); 0 mg Cholesterol; 22 g Carbohydrate (3 g Fibre, 8 g Sugar); 4 g Protein; 440 mg Sodium

Vichyssoise

This chilled potato and leek soup is an international favourite. It's wonderful for a casual summer dinner or as an elegant addition to a fancier feast.

Butter (or hard margarine)	2 tsp.	10 mL
Sliced leek (white part only)	1 1/2 cups	375 mL
Chopped onion	1/2 cup	125 mL
Dried thyme	1/4 tsp.	1 mL
Prepared chicken (or vegetable) broth	3 cups	750 mL
Chopped peeled potato	1 1/2 cups	375 mL
Bay leaf	1	1
Salt	1/4 tsp.	1 mL
Cayenne pepper	1/8 tsp.	0.5 mL
Half-and-half cream (or homogenized milk)	1/2 cup	125 mL
Chopped fresh chives, for garnish		

Melt butter in a large saucepan on medium. Add next 3 ingredients. Cook for 5 to 10 minutes, stirring often, until leek and onion are softened.

Stir in next 5 ingredients and bring to a boil. Reduce heat to medium. Boil gently, uncovered, for 15 to 20 minutes, stirring occasionally, until potato is tender. Remove and discard bay leaf. Following manufacturer's instructions for processing hot liquids, carefully process with a hand blender, or in a blender in batches, until smooth.

Add cream. Stir well. Transfer to a large bowl and let cool at room temperature before covering. Chill for at least 2 hours until cold. Garnish individual servings with chives. Makes about 5 cups (1.25 L).

1 cup (250 mL): 110 Calories; 4 g Total Fat (0 g Mono, 0 g Poly, 2.5 g Sat); 15 mg Cholesterol; 16 g Carbohydrate (2 g Fibre, 4 g Sugar); 2 g Protein; 720 mg Sodium

Melon Berry Soup

The colours in this vibrant soup excite the eye and the palate. Serve in chilled bowls for a light, refreshing dessert on a hot summer evening.

Chopped ripe cantaloupe	5 cups	1.25 L
White grape juice	1 cup	250 mL
Lemon juice	2 tbsp.	30 mL
Fresh (or frozen, thawed) raspberries	1 1/2 cups	375 mL
White grape juice	1/3 cup	75 mL

Process first 3 ingredients in a blender or food processor until smooth. Transfer to a medium bowl.

Process raspberries and second amount of grape juice in a blender or food processor until smooth. Strain through a sieve into a small bowl. Discard seeds. Stir into cantaloupe mixture. Chill, covered, for at least 2 hours until cold. Makes 6 servings.

1 serving: 110 Calories; 4 g Total Fat (0 g Mono, 0 g Poly, 2.5 g Sat); 15 mg Cholesterol; 16 g Carbohydrate (2 g Fibre, 4 g Sugar); 2 g Protein; 720 mg Sodium

∾ White grape juice is not as well known as its purple counterpart, but it is readily available in supermarkets and online. It is made from green grapes instead of red and is significantly sweeter than regular grape juice.

Pineapple Mango Soup

This sweet treat makes a perfect palate cleanser or a refreshing dessert. Serve in punch cups and drizzle with coconut milk and minced strawberries for extra style points.

Cans of sliced mango (with syrup), (14 oz., 398 mL, each)	2	2
Chopped fresh pineapple	6 cups	1.5 L
Coconut milk	1/2 cup	125 mL

Process all 3 ingredients in a blender or food processor until smooth. Press through a sieve into a large bowl. Discard solids. Chill, covered, for at least 2 hours until cold. Makes about 6 cups (1.5 L).

1 cup (250 mL): 210 Calories; 4 g Total Fat (0 g Mono, 0 g Poly, 3.5 g Sat); 0 mg Cholesterol; 43 g Carbohydrate (3 g Fibre, 35 g Sugar); 1 g Protein; 20 mg Sodium

Pineapples do not continue to ripen once they have been picked, so you want to make sure you buy one that is already ripe. When shopping for a whole pineapple, look for one that is plump and heavy for its size, with fresh green leaves. The skin of pineapples can be green or yellow and the colour does not reflect the ripeness of the fruit, so don't be fooled into thinking yellow skin is better. Instead, smell the bottom of pineapple; a ripe pineapple will have a fresh, strong pineapple scent. When squeezed, the pineapple should have only a little bit of give. If it is soft, it has passed its prime.

Strawberry Rhubarb Soup

Never wonder what you're going to do with your bounty of garden rhubarb again! The sweet and sour flavours of strawberry and rhubarb mingle with citrusy orange to make a lovely fine-weather treat. Garnish each serving with a small dollop of whipping cream.

Water	2 cups	500 mL
Granulated sugar	3/4 cup	175 mL
Chopped frozen (or fresh) rhubarb	2 cups	500 mL
Chopped frozen (or fresh) strawberries	4 cups	1 L
Orange juice	1 1/4 cups	300 mL
Whipping cream (or half-and-half cream), for garnish		

Bring water and sugar to a boil in a large saucepan, stirring occasionally. Add rhubarb and reduce heat to medium. Boil gently, covered, for about 5 minutes until rhubarb is softened.

Stir in strawberries and orange juice. Cook for 2 to 3 minutes, stirring occasionally, until strawberries are softened. Remove from heat. Following manufacturer's instructions for processing hot liquids, carefully process with a hand blender, or in a blender in batches, until smooth. Transfer to a medium bowl. Cool at room temperature before covering. Chill for at least 2 hours until cold.

Top individual servings with a small dollop of whipping cream. Makes about 4 1/2 cups (1.1 L).

1 cup (250 mL): 220 Calories; .5 g Total Fat (0 g Mono, 0 g Poly, 0 g Sat); 0 mg Cholesterol; 54 g Carbohydrate (4 g Fibre, 41 g Sugar); 2 g Protein; 0 mg Sodium

Index